the praise

"*City Chic* is an absolute joy to read! It is chock full of clever, unconventional tips about how to cheat your way to a stylish life without spending a lot of money."

—Barbara Corcoran, author of *Use What You've Got, and Other Business Lessons I Learned From My Mom*

"Who needs self-help books? With Nina Willdorf's tips for living (well) on less, you're guaranteed to dress better, have a nicer apartment, learn how to cook and dumpster dive, and probably be happier, too. Essential reading for the 'poverty elite.'"

—Lucinda Rosenfeld, author of *What She Saw...*

"Living in New York on a budget has been a long-time focus of mine. This book is key to survival in the Big Apple, and no woman should leave home without it."

—Lucy Barnes, fashion designer

"I LOVE the book. If only I've had it for the past ten years— it would've saved me lots of heartache, bad furniture, and, most importantly, money....It gives you license to scrimp and pinch—and makes you feel empowered to do so."

—Gigi Guerra, *Lucky* magazine

"Willdorf elevates penny pinching to an art form. *City Chic* is constantly inventive, amazingly granular, and a blast to read."

—Dany Levy, founder/chairman, DailyCandy, Inc.

city chic

NINA WILLDORF

an urban girl's guide to livin' large on less

SOURCEBOOKS, INC.
NAPERVILLE, ILLINOIS

Published by Sourcebooks, Inc.
P.O. Box 4410, Naperville, Illinois 60567-4410
(630) 961-3900 • FAX: (630) 961-2168
www.sourcebooks.com

Library of Congress Cataloging-in-Publication Data
Willldorf, Nina.
  City chic : an urban girl's guide to livin' large on less / by Nina Willldorf.
      p. cm.
Includes index.
  ISBN 1-4022-0054-4
  1. Young women—Life skills guides. 2. Young women—Finance,
Personal. I. Title.
HQ1229 .W73 2003
646.7'0084'22—dc21   2003153629

Printed and bound in the United States of America
ED   10   9

the thanks

An Urban Girl is nothing without her cheerleaders, her mentors, her family, and her friends. From the pals who provided nuggets of inspiration to the patient folks who fielded panicky phone calls to the corps who devoted much time and red pen ink to the cause, I am genuinely indebted; this book has been a true team effort.

First off, I must thank Michael Endelman, without whose tireless support, enthusiasm, and delicious dinners I would be a sad sack of a girl. Seth Gitell must be credited for planting the germ of an idea for this book, on a late afternoon session of career talk over bad coffee. And yes, introducing me to the best agent a girl could ever hope for, Andrew Stuart, who has acted above and beyond as an editor, champion, and friend. My family, for fielding an endless stream of angst. Sari Globerman, for being my confidante, editor, therapist, and the bestest friend a girl could have. Jennifer Fusco and the Sourcebooks team, for taking a leap of faith and believing in me.

Girls (and a few boys) who generously permitted me to sift through the contents of their brains and share their ingenious methods include the alarmingly talented Jane Ko, Tracie Egan, Debbie Stoller, Lisa Keys, Jeannie Christensen, Dina Cheney, the Wish girls in Boston, Moxie's Karen, Sandra Kang, Summer McClinton, the indomitable Douglas Fitch, Caroline Pam, and Sarah Lydon, among many others who know who they are. The most sincere of thanks to Jill Davis, for getting it and sharing priceless pieces of advice; the inspiringly inquisitive Susan Orlean, and the warmest of the warm, Wendy Wasserstein—for generously sharing your stories and reminisces.

Then there are the experts who make this whole enterprise legit: the boundlessly delightful Sheryl Julian; textile geniuses Katherine Hatch and

Janice Stone; plant and flower guru Bill Epstein, the Nurseryman's Exchange; beauty pro Karmen Butterer; Color Association of the U.S.'s Margaret Walch; Boston Sports Club's Danielle Abrams; super sweet and stylish Elisabeth Filarski; and the smart, sassy, stylish Louis Boston's Debi Greenberg, whose passion for the cause I can only hope to approximate in the future.

Finally, to Lisa Gerson and Emily Parker, for devoting hours of their precious time reading the roughest of drafts—and whom I trust completely to be mercifully honest, *merci*.

the urban girl's cheat sheet

section 4: wear

introduction

Here you are, getting started on your career in the big city.

With a brain full of big ideas, you dropped down with a sparkling vision of your future. There will be fancy fêtes, fresh flowers placed throughout a light, airy apartment, gourmet dinners prepared on an industrial range, a closet full of chic, clean garments, time to spare, and ladders to climb. Ahh, the good life.

Err. But, you soon realize, it's not quite that rosy in the real world.

You may be bursting with ideas, but you're short on cash. Your taste buds are primed four stars, but your cupboards echo when you open them. You eagerly pore over stylized glossy pages in *Vogue* and then peer down at your dragging, frayed hemlines. You longingly flip through *Elle Décor* and then glance around at your peeling wallpaper and chipped paint. You devoutly read page after page of *Yoga Journal* and then take stock of your soft, fleshy body.

Welcome to your Fiscally Challenged twenties and thirties. You know you're a member of the Fiscally Challenged Club when, despite a healthy dose of pride in your work, the accompanying paycheck can only be described as, well, *slim*. You avoid peeking at your monthly balance in your bank statement. You mentally clock how much you'll have left over after devoting 50 percent of your income to rent. And you dream of the day when picking up mail won't be a matter of dread (cable bill, credit card bill, nasty note from landlord, cell phone bill, yikes); when dinner out with friends won't be an obstacle course of mental calculations [*Should you order another drink (+$6)? Who wants dessert (+$10)*]; when an afternoon of shopping will include more than peering longingly through windows.

You have desires for certain hemlines, bedspreads, and glassware—big ones! But whether or not you can afford it all now, you don't give up hope. Money may be an object, but you refuse to let it be an obstacle. That's because what you may lack in funds, you make up in daring and desire.

While your budget may be more Nordstrom's than Neiman's, more Banana Republic than Barneys, more Gap than Gucci, you're intent on looking as snazzy as money-dropping Madonna. You're the kind of girl who knows that all it takes to make cubic zirconium come off as D-grade diamonds is a certain amount of conviction. And, fortunately, conviction and poise come cheap.

Think of it as your big secret, your way of creatively cheating at looking chic. Call it the New Thrift. And unlike the Salvation Army clothing you fancied as *edgy* in high school, this thrift is more glam than grunge, more good-looking than Goodwill.

It sure sounds good, right? But how do you look like a million bucks for more like $150? Learning how to live just as well for less money is a lifelong project, one that requires equal measures of inventiveness, skill, and savvy. Instead of wallowing in what you can't have, you take pride in the *get*, the deals, and the accompanying stories. Your closet is a picturebook of finds. Your kitchen a scrapbook-to-be of fun meals with your friends. Your bathroom a laboratory of dimestore fare dressed up in shiny bottles.

Allow me to chart the Urban Girl's cost-conscious course. This is a subject I've been immersed in over the course of four pay cuts, five cities, and more bounced checks than I'd like to admit. I am a journalist who covers lifestyle issues for magazines and newspapers. It is my job to inform readers of deals, strategies, and inspiring ways other women have lived well on their scant salaries. In the process of writing about stylish savings, I've lived it as well.

I started this book when I graduated from college in 1999. But even then, I didn't know it was a book. It was simply the way I found myself living; information that I compiled out of necessity; sneaky savings strategies to attain the life that my friends and I were all striving for.

To complicate things, as I moved up in my field, looking good became an integral part of my job, a goal that became increasingly hard to achieve.

There were dinners to be had, wines to be tasted, shoes to be purchased, eyebrows to be waxed. And with my small salaries, I had to come up with some sneaky savings alternatives, devising ways to do it for less. Certainly, I flailed at the beginning—dressing too casually; allowing too much time between haircuts; blindly ordering the wrong thing and paying the price, literally.

I figured there had to be something I didn't know about, a clue that all of my fellow low-rungers held that allowed them to make similarly low salaries yet enabled them to maintain wonderfully stylish appearances. I needed to know what it was. Thus, awash in an equal number of bills, clothing catalogs, and bright ideas, I began my training and informal research for this book.

Perhaps the cause of my tight budget was my living situation. So, to save money initially, I lived with my parents, with friends of my parents, with people I didn't know, and with roommates whose idea of cleaning was sweeping moldy Hot Tamales under the futon—all in the name of low rent. But there needed to be a better answer, a way to have the life I wanted without reclaiming my high school bedroom.

So I tried some new thrift techniques. At first they were cautious and simple. I got cable and stayed home. I invested in a cookbook that featured dinners made on a scant three ingredients. I bought only generic items and packed a lunch. I started training for a marathon—a cheap way to stay in shape, and a great way to spend time without spending too much money! It became my excuse not to drink away $20 on Friday night, which is *far* too easy. "I have to run eighteen miles tomorrow," I'd offer, only half-apologetically. People started looking at me as if I were insane. And with good reason. Obviously, this was not the life I dreamed of.

Then, when early spring rolled around, I did a freelance assignment and set aside the money for a fabulous pair of winter shoes. Rather than buy the twill skirt I wanted for spring, I bought the BCBG black calf-hugging leather boots that would still be fabulous next winter. I developed a style that could only be described as daringly eclectic, as I gathered more and more items like my now-coveted kicks. Pink flooded corduroys? They became my signature spunky fall look.

Inspiration comes in unlikely forms. I saw my eighty-two-year-old grandmother carry a twenty-year-old beige LeSportsac shoulder bag. I marveled at how good and stylish it looked in a clunky utilitarian way. And what longevity! I bought one and never let it leave my side. I got my hair cut dramatically short, and the salon showed me how to style it so I wouldn't have to come back for five months. Eventually, after noting how well I was doing with my new savings techniques, I even indulged in a pricey leather Miu Miu shoulder bag, which was still far over-budget even after a hefty Filene's Basement markdown.

And as I started to look the part, I realized I wanted to play the part, too. I felt increasingly confident about the possibilities of my new lifestyle. My boots were itching for an unveiling, my bag begging for a viewing. I chased my eighteen-mile dusk workouts with marathon sessions of cocktails and realized I'd rather sip one Makers Mark Manhattan straight up than swill numerous Rolling Rocks. I wouldn't hesitate to join girlfriends at a pricey bistro; instead of a $30 sirloin steak, I'd simply opt for an $18 vegetarian pasta dish. And now that I could spend my Friday evenings enjoying fine food and drink, I needed a fitness option other than prohibitively expensive $15 yoga classes. So I invested in a workout video.

In short, I took it on as my second job to hone the craft of living well for less. And best of all, I found it to be fun. My salary may have been an embarrassment, but I wouldn't let my life be the same. For the most part, the building of my low-budget high-style life resembled a game show—supermarket sweep for the stylishly inclined. How low could I go? Economizing became something of an exuberant challenge. Grocery shopping turned into a sport as I trolled around looking for the cheapest price, tallying weights and comparing labels. Decorating my apartment was an obstacle course, requiring pluck, resourcefulness, and a willingness to form some blisters.

As I advanced in my pursuit, the challenges became more complex. Finally, I conquered The Dinner Party, which combined everything I'd previously shied away from: cost and culinary skill. I cohosted an evening with a girlfriend—she was responsible for appetizers and wine, I managed everything else. It was a blast. Sitting around the table, surrounded by friends and friends of friends, the ladies started expounding on their own versions of tips, their own cost-saving secrets. Kerry's was never buying wine by the glass at a restaurant. Megan avoided reupholstering furniture by tying high-thread-count sheets over her chairs with demure bows at the legs. My friends were fonts of inspiration and encouraged me to discover the myriad ways life can be lived in high style at low cost.

The next step was simply sharing the information with women like you.

Over the course of writing this book, I've found folks who take equal pleasure in this quest. Through numerous interviews with friends, clothing buyers, style gurus, foodies, and financial whizzes, I've assembled a selective and thorough road map for girls with a desire for the stylish life and a cap on their credit card limits. We are in good company!

Soon enough, you too will be saving money on haircuts, you will be able to recite the essential kitchen ingredients to throw a last-minute low-budget soiree, you will know instinctively how to remove that splash of wine from your favorite pair of pants, you will be able to toss off the secret words to get a deal on your gym membership.

Consider *City Chic* your low-budget high-style bible, your point of inspiration, your guide to the good life at low cost. It is the assistant's right-hand cheat sheet, the artist's secret weapon, the student's primer. An Urban Girl's best friend.

THIS URBAN GIRL'S FINANCES

Don't just take my word for it. Conduct an audit on my finances while I open up my checkbook to demonstrate just how I lived in style on a budget while writing this very book.

From April 2002 to September 2002, I lived on a combination of a salary from the *Boston Phoenix* ($24,000/year—so low!), where I was a staff writer, and freelance income from *Glamour* magazine and other publications ($5,000 over six months), and this book advance ($5,000). While my income varied from month to month, I generally had a little over $2,000 a month to play with after taxes.

Here's how I made the most of my bank account

Rent: $500–$800 a month (my boyfriend Michael and I lived in a wonderfully cheap, railroad-style, one-bedroom apartment in Cambridge, and then we sublet an apartment on the Upper West Side of Manhattan for the summer. Following that, we found a lovely one-bedroom apartment in the East Village. Sure, we lucked out, but it just goes to show that you can find deals everywhere. We found them in two of the most expensive cities in the country!)

Utilities: $40–$50 a month (to save a little here and there, I reach for the tank tops in summer and cozy sweaters in winter, rather than the thermostat. It all adds up!)

Groceries: $150–$200 a month (I splurge on groceries and buy the best fruits and vegetables so that I can eat in. An empty fridge means more meals out = $$$)

Laundry/Dry Cleaning: $20 a month (whenever possible, I hand wash)

Communications: $45 (cell phone) + $21.95 (internet access) + $40 (long distance) +30 (local plan) = $136.95

Transportation: $80–$100 a month (this figure includes public transportation and a few cabs or car expenses, when we still had one. I like to buy monthly passes as incentive to take public transportation rather than splurging on cabs)

Entertainment: $60 (cable) + $150 in cover charges, concert tickets, and movies

Dining out: $100 a month (I like to spend a lot on a couple of great meals a month rather than go out for a bunch of just OK $20 dinners)

Gym membership: $60 a month (I said I was a student. *Shhh!*)

Personal maintenance: $50 a month (including haircuts, occasional manicure/pedicure splurges, waxing)

Clothes: $200 a month (or, whatever's left over)

Total: $1,926 (with a little left over for savings!)

HOME
section one

chapter one

lighten up

"There is no such thing as an ugly color. There is such a thing as an ugly color combination."

—Douglas Fitch, artist and interior designer in New York

i went to college in New York City, where a shoebox-sized room is considered ample space. Housing in college anywhere in the country is already a less-than-luxurious affair, with twin beds and utilitarian design. But in converted New York apartment buildings, dusty and musty and crumbling and full of *(ahem)* character, the dorms I lived in required some serious savvy decorating skills. Each year, as I crossed the threshold into my new space, depositing boxes of books and bedding, I surveyed the design challenges, the many limitations, and the even more bountiful options to make things fabulous. New year, new apartment, new creative challenges.

First, there was a modernist cube cinderblock room I shared with my roommate Adrianne. We had two twin beds, an elaborate shelving unit occupying one wall, and a floor of cool linoleum. We lay down rugs, hung disguising wall hangings over the oppressively drab cinderblock, used soft lamps, and formed an "ahhh" nest.

Later, I shared a studio apartment with Julia. It was also dorm housing, but in a converted prewar apartment building owned by the university. When I moved in, there was a bunk bed hugging one wall, two dressers in the middle of the room, and a kitchen that could fit one person (as long as she sucked in and angled in sideways). Things looked bleak. But we went to work. The first thing we did was separate the bunk bed—*I mean, really, how old were we?* Then we pushed a worn-out couch below the windows at the head of the room, which we covered in a beautiful, purple-hued Indian spread. Candles and lighting touches clinched the transition from drab dorm to cozy casa.

Over the course of the next few years, I cultivated essential skills, such as sprucing up a room with a perfectly placed plant, devising slipcovers for well-worn furniture, and hanging just the right number of pictures on the wall to create "cozy" without getting "claustrophobic."

I saw: A crevice of a foyer. **It became:** an "office."

I saw: A blank wall. **It became:** a shelving unit for kitchen wares that don't fit in the two cabinets.

I saw: a window that faced anything other than a brick wall. **It became:** a focal point of the apartment, enhanced by a hanging plant.

I saw: a doorframe. **It became:** the ideal spot to hang hooks for coats.

Everything multitasks, and anything that's not a problem becomes a potential boon.

As an Urban Girl, you find yourself in similar decorating predicaments. Small apartments and shares are bursting with creative challenges; you rise to them with gusto, rubbing your hands in anticipation, your eyes darting around to scope all the ins and outs of your space. Everything—everything—has potential. A folding screen becomes a door between a "convertible two bedroom." Stacks of books act as a makeshift coffee table. A stepstool doubles as a pedestal for a droopy plant. You can make something out of anything. Hit the ground running.

COLOR

First and foremost in your apartment transformation is painting. There's no better way to transform your space, to make it yours, than to throw some color on the walls. And as far as apartment renovations go, painting is an affordable way to make your space better—especially if you do it yourself. You're not ripping out walls (please), you're not installing appliances (1-800-HELP-MOI), but you're completely comfortable taking on a good paint job. All you have to invest in are a few cans of paint, some brushes and rollers, and a six-pack of beer to lure your friends over to make a day of it.

TIP: word to the wise

If your landlord doesn't allow painting, don't worry. Every apartment I've ever lived in has the clause in the lease that you're not allowed to paint. Ignore it. It's likely that the next tenant will be stunned by your impeccable taste and choose to keep the color anyway. And if not, in many states, your landlord would be required to slap on another coat of white before having the new tenant move in. The worst-case scenario is that you have to paint over your color. In that case, meet Kilz, a primer that covers up even the brightest bordello red. Consider the color dead.

Chances are, when you first move in, your apartment will be white. If you're lucky, you may have started off with something a little spicier, like eggshell or a very pale crème. But none of those will do as the sole color for the entire home. All-white walls, like an all-white wardrobe, are too easy, and they waste precious creative space. You should leave no more than one room in your home in plain ol' white. It will act as a pause between your other rooms. While wild color combinations (yellow and green and red, all at once!) may be a bad idea, every single room in white does nothing for you. At the very least, brush on an eggshell or a pale gray.

Identify your room needs

Before you go slapping up a shocking shade of orange in your bedroom, you will need to figure out exactly what you require from each room. Does your bedroom double as a study? Do you enjoy reading the newspaper at your kitchen table in the mornings? Is your bathroom a beautifying space? All of the colors you choose will help make your home well-suited to your exact housing needs.

Separating Space: Most Urban Girls are still in situations that are, generously speaking, a little humble: sharing apartments or living in cramped studios or one-bedrooms. Paint can work wonderfully in small starter apartments by clearly delineating space and creating the illusion of vastness.

My boyfriend Michael and I moved into a very small railroad-style one-bedroom in Cambridge a couple of years ago. There were no doors between the rooms, and, well, even using the word "room" could be considered generous. A very tall person lying down could probably have a limb in three "rooms" at once. Needless to say, we had to find a way to make the space seem larger. It was the first time that we had lived together, and it was the first time either of us had shacked up with a significant other. We were both nervous about having enough personal space and personal time. So making our small apartment seem larger was key.

To that end, we painted the bedroom and the living room a pale blue-gray, keeping the door frames white, and we painted the kitchen and bathroom a sunny shade of yellow, leaving the study white. Walking from room to room after we'd painted really felt like transitioning from one space to another, just because of the color. We could be in different "rooms," and even though there weren't doors, we could still feel like we were in another part of the house.

In a small apartment, use different colors in different rooms to make each its own space and make the apartment seem more spacious.

Haven homes

If you live in any city, from New York to Chicago, San Francisco to Boston, Los Angeles to Washington, D.C., your apartment must provide a space of respite, of soothing calm. Coming home is your chance to get away from car alarms, smelly curb-side trash, and whistling construction workers. Again, the perfectly suited wall color can make your apartment into a blissful zen space that envelops you in a warm hug as you cross the threshold. Ahhh....

Sun shockers

You're a lucky girl if you wake up to sun streaming through your windows. Or you come home to late-afternoon light filtering through your window shades. Nothing makes me feel better than curling up in an armchair, bathed in late-morning sun. Bliss. But sometimes, an affordable apartment isn't a sunny one. Sometimes, light is something you have to coax out, through small windows, slats of lights. If your apartment is bright and south facing, you'll want to paint your walls in cool colors that enhance the light. If it's north facing, you'll need to coax out the brightness. A pale yellow or an eggshell is a great shade to enhance light in dark or basement apartments.

What to do where?

Once you've decided to take the color plunge, choosing the perfect shade for each room and considering your needs becomes important. Any old color won't do in any old room. To fulfill your requirements, you'll need to make sure you choose the right color for each space. Luckily, there are some hard and fast rules from color experts and interior designers about what works where, so you needn't stand aimlessly with a full palate, dizzy with too many choices.

Red
Good in: dining room, family room, library, dressing room, entryway
Avoid in: bedroom, bathroom
Makes you want to: get creative, do wild things, be the next MTV VJ
The message: Yowza

Yellow
Good in: closet, kitchen, bathroom
Avoid in: study, living room
Makes you want to: cook, sweep, be a domestic goddess
The message: Ahh

Pale Charcoal
Good in: bedroom, entryway
Avoid in: kitchen, study, bathroom
Makes you want to: relax, treat yourself right, read, light candles, return
    phone calls
The message: Yawn

Light blue
Good in: bedroom, living room, entryway
Avoid in: kitchen
Makes you want to: chill, curl up in a rocking chair,
    write letters
The message: Purr

Lime green
Good in: bathrooms, hallways
Avoid in: everywhere else
Makes you want to: experiment with funky new
    looks, tweeze, cleanse, and try new shades of
    lipstick
The message: Hmm...

who knew?
Blue is supposedly an
appetite suppressant,
reported *House &
Garden*. Do you really
want that in your
kitchen?

Boxed in to four walls? Think again

Tackling an entire apartment with tarps, cans of paint, and a host of brushes can seem like a mammoth task. But who said you had to paint all four walls and the ceiling in order to redecorate your apartment?

Sometimes, to save money and time, or to boost originality, it pays to think outside the four-walls box.

Think accent

An accent wall is simply one wall of a room painted a wash of color. When my roommate Lisa and I moved into our first apartment in Boston, which was all white, we were looking to paint one wall in the living room a daring, fun color. The wall in question was opposite four windows and would house a tan-striped couch. "Red," I exclaimed. "Is the perfect color for this wall."

Lisa was a little cautious about explosive red, so we finally settled on a pomegranate shade the paint company called "Tahiti." How festive! With the first roll up on the wall, we paused and looked at each other with raised eyebrows and open lips over clenched teeth. Yikes. It was really bright. But there was no turning back now. After three coats, we were done. We had a bold red wall that won many a compliment over the next year and did us many party favors.

Painting four walls Tahiti would have been a bit much, but one stand-alone wall had a unique, tempered, and still stylish effect. Also, only painting one wall was both a cost-saving trick (buy less paint) and shaved hours off the time it took us to get the job done (you spend a quarter of the time). But better than all those boons was the fact that the one wall provided an edge to our otherwise demure apartment. It became our signature.

Think doors and frames

When painting an entire room, including door frames—or not—can drastically change the effect. If you'd like to keep the apartment all white, consider painting just the doors or the door frames. Like the inviting whimsy of a front door painted red, a painted door or door frame in an apartment can also provide a unique touch. Just be sure to unify colors. Don't go

who knew?

painting one frame one color and the door in another room another. You're aiming for simplicity here.

Think moldings, trim, and fireplaces

Similarly, choose a color to paint the molding of your room, if you're lucky enough to have such a touch in your apartment. My mother enjoys bright, cheery colors, and when working with a designer on a palate for the entryway and living room to my parents' house, she indulged her appreciation for all things colorful—a little blue here, a couple shades of yellow there, trim in gray. The effect is striking. And it certainly works because there's enough space. But in a smaller apartment, or one with less light, it's more important to consider a color scheme for the entire space, colors that complement each other. Moldings and trim are an easy way to add some attitude to your apartment without spending too much time and money on supplies.

Small room, big ideas

Your room may be eight by ten and your apartment may be 400 square feet, but the beauty of painting is the ability to make it turn into a palace, your very own oddly expansive funhouse. Follow these rules to create the illusion of turning your 400 square feet into 1000.

Proportional thinking (60/30/10)

To enlarge a small room, go easy on crazy color combinations. Your wall color should occupy 60 percent of the color in the room; the furniture, rugs, and window treatments should take up no more than 30 percent of the color; and accents, such as books, pillows, and hangings should be no more than 10 percent.

Wall strategy

In a small, square room, paint two opposite walls the same color. The space will have the illusion of being much deeper than it is. Another option is to paint the ceiling a lighter shade to make it seem higher than it is.

Color blues

The color blue has the helpful effect of making a small room seem to expand. It provides the illusion of height. Maybe it's because of blue skies.

LIGHTING

Nothing makes me shudder more than a houseguest marching into my kitchen, reaching for a chain hanging from the ceiling, and tugging it down in a firm and decisive *thwap* to turn on the overhead light. *Noooooo*, I rush over, turning it off, and heading for the halogen in the corner. It's like I'm the wicked witch and I'm *meeeeelllllting*. The light zaps all my mojo. Whatever the apartment, whatever the room, the overhead lighting that's been provided just will not do. It bathes the apartment in a dull, depressing thin light that neither illuminates nor flatters. And really, where's the upside of that?

who knew?
Lighting can account for as much as 25 percent of your electricity bill. Choose your methods wisely and you can reduce that percentage and see your bills shrink.

Light up your life

Lighting offers wonderful opportunities to change a mood. You can go from bright and cheery to mellow and slow to sleepy and seductive, all by simply using a different bulb, a well-angled lamp, or—err—nothing at all. There are many different options, but there is only one rule: ditch the overhead lights. You can find truly terrific lamps for cheap, or you can make your own lampshades easily.

Four different basic kinds of lighting

Fluorescent

The thin bars, usually covered by thin sheaths of beveled plastic, spread their flickering, headache-inducing light in most cheaply done office buildings, parking garages, and elementary schools. Under no circumstance should the Urban Girl use a fluorescent light. She will not look nearly the beauty she is under the pallor of such a glare. Though fluorescent bulbs are the most energy-efficient available, she never sacrifices emotional well-being for saving a buck.

Halogen

A bright, focused light, halogen works well for adding a focus to tasks that require fine concentration. Reading before bed, writing letters, sewing on buttons, tweezing, painting nails. Basically, anything where you're going for precision and attentiveness can be well served with a halogen. Halogen lights are generally more expensive than incandescent and fluorescent, though a good incandescent can spread a similar, centered brightness that gets the job done at a lower price. Halogens are the second-most energy-efficient bulbs; they use 20 percent less energy than incandescent and generally last for two thousand to six thousand hours. Plenty!

Incandescent

Incandescent lights are basically what you think of when you envision light bulbs. They're the pear-shaped numbers with the little wire in the middle. Not the long tubes of fluorescent, not the short cylinders of halogen, incandescent lighting is made up of small bulbs that cast a wide, softer, yellow light. You can choose a variety of bulbs that will vary the ultimate effect of this kind of light. These are the least energy-efficient kind of bulbs because the light is cast so wide. Only 5 percent of energy used goes toward light, while the rest of the energy goes toward casting heat. Good for the winter.

Candles

They often smell good, they flicker, they provide vibe, and they're a reliable option that works when electricity doesn't. Candles are a win-win lighting alternative and can be employed everywhere from the bathroom to the kitchen to the living room. Typing away on a rainy Sunday? Light a softly scented candle. Having a party and want to keep the bathroom lit without the harsh overhead? Leave a few candles on the sink and counter. Having a dinner party and want to transform the kitchen table from bustling to decadent? Lace the table with dozens of floating candles. Best of all, after the initial investment, candles are free and require no energy.

Kinds of lamps

When choosing what will work best in lieu of overhead light bulbs (always a bad idea), you have a number of options. Each casts a different glow.

Desk

A desk lamp has a limited span but casts a round light on a set area.
Use if: concentrating on one task
Avoid if: reading

Floor

A floor lamp has a more dispersed light. Try one with three settings to provide the most alternatives, or one with three different heads you can angle in various ways.
Use if: lighting a room
Avoid if: reading

Room needs

Depending on exactly what you're doing at the time, each room of your apartment can change from chill to concentrate mode, from relaxation to rarin' to go.

It's so easy. You can just use your lighting to change the mood. Here's a room-by-room guide on the best ways to increase your options, using just a different lamp, a well-placed candle, or nothing at all.

Kitchen

For cooking: a halogen light, on high, in the corner
For dinner parties: a table full of floating candles, with the halogen (or incandescent) on low
For cleaning: a halogen or incandescent light on high, to detect and lasso all the dust bunnies possible
For Sunday morning newspaper reading: window shades pulled up and candles for brightest setting

Bedroom

For reading: a halogen aimed down to the page or a bright incandescent angled to the wall right behind your head, to reflect onto the page
For hanky panky: candles and lots of 'em
For cooling off after a long, hard day pounding the pavement: a mix of candles and low light

Study

For paying bills: an incandescent or halogen desk lamp
For typing/reading/working: same, plus a candle for scented inspiration
For procrastinating: candles and no light

who knew?

Spritz a little whiff of perfume or cologne onto a light bulb. Just a little. As the bulb warms, the scent will spread around and fill the room, providing a similar effect to a scented candle.

TIP: best bulbs for various rendezvous

Yellow bulbs: Dinner parties, quiet evenings at home
White bulbs: Office meetings, house cleaning
Black bulbs: Intense conversations

Living room
For watching television: floor lamp in corner on mid-to-low level
For reading: swivel halogen lamp pointed to the page
For hanging out with friends: candles and floor lamp on medium or low, depending on if they're friends or "friends"

who knew?
Have a harsh bulb or lamp that you'd rather not invest in replacing? Angle the light toward the wall or a corner of the room, upward. The light will deflect and spread, becoming warmer.

chapter two

furnish for less

"Buying a couch—that was a big thing! But you do have to have a comfortable place you can sit."

—Wendy Wasserstein, playwright and author of *Shiksa Goddess,* on her first furniture investment out of graduate school

You've moved in. You've mapped out the lay of the land. You've dusted down the walls, primed and painted, and turned the white canvas of your pre-adorned apartment into a bright, airy space. Brava. But before you plop down on the floor, pooped, the games have only just begun. Now, you get to become the architect of your own lair.

SETTLING ON A SCHEME

When setting out to furnish your pad, it's important to decide ahead of time what *look* you're going for. Mixing up country ruffles with minimalist chrome and earthy Pottery Barn will simply make a mishmash out of your decorating scheme.

Depending on your personality, you will gravitate toward one aesthetic or another. Remember, whatever you do, stick to the plan. A funky array of disjointed furniture says "student"; we're going for Aspiring Adult here.

Minimalist

The minimalist home is straight out of a Calvin Klein ad in a glossy magazine. Grays blend into blacks, contrast with whites, crèmes, and chromes. Everything is square, rectangle, perfectly aligned, and well spaced out. The minimalist decorator comes home and immediately lights a tall beige candle, which sits atop stacks of coffee-table books and emits a steady kiss of fragrance. She removes shoes and putters around on a thin charcoal wool rug.

Country Home

The country home lady loves a little ruffle here and there. And really, who can blame her? Throughout her apartment, she throws together cheery gingham and yellows, along with wood furniture. It's Dolly Parton meets Beaver Cleaver.

Uptown Old World

The uptown lady has a thing for antiques. She loves the look of a richly patterned oriental rug, which sits under many a well-lacquered piece of cherry furniture. Every item is a "piece," and *everything* has a story.

Au Naturale

The au naturale decorator can't get enough of earth tones. The browns, the army greens, the beiges. They all mix together under many a hanging plant to create the illusion of being in thick woods.

Southwestern

The southwestern lady feels a little spicy and individualistic. Where better to present that image to the world than in her home, where she throws together Mexican print patterns, heavy wood tables, and stenciled walls. *Olé!*

Look before you leap

Whatever look you decide on, the most important thing you can do at this point is **slow down, killer**. One more night sleeping on the futon will pay off when you score a prize-winning bed. Plunk down the plastic for the first dining room table you see—impractically scratched glass, gauche design, and all—and you're living with it until you can afford to replace it. Move in Monday and expect to have everything perfectly arranged by Saturday? You're setting yourself up for settling on stuff that's not quite right, not the best price, and not a good idea!

KNOW WHEN TO NEGOTIATE

If you thought markups were inexplicably high in the retail clothing world, just wait till you start pricing couches. In his authoritative book, *Shopping for Furniture: A Consumer's Guide*, Leonard Bruce Lewin reveals that furniture stores generally mark up their merchandise by two to three times what the retailer paid for it. Two to three times! Don't get caught red-handed as a **sticker price sucker**, taking the printed dollar signs as set in stone.

Percentage versus dollars

When in doubt, keep an eye on the percentage markdown. When dealing with furniture, fifteen percent is often gratuitous. Aim for anything higher than a 25 to 30 percent markdown. Once you get above that limit, you can start deciding among furniture treasures. A 60 percent-off ottoman may be super cheap, but the 30 percent-off one is far superior. Go with your gut after you get above the 30 percent barrier.

Bargaining power

A big store may not negotiate prices, but if you're in love with an item, and it's double the price you had planned on spending, bust out your bargaining chips. Ask them for a discount on a second item, or to include delivery charges in the price. The only way you can be sure you *won't* get a deal is if you don't ask at all!

DEALS, DEALS, DEALS!

While buying retail is tempting in furnishing your place—*only the best!*— here is one area where the best deals are found second- or third-hand. You'll find solid wares that have barely been used for prices you can toast to. Scour the stores and come home a winner, arms a-pumpin' Rocky-style.

Antiques

You may think antiquing (yes, it's a verb) is only for single old ladies, residents of New England, and Christie's devotees, but thrifty, stylish Urban Girls will find that it's a minefield for major furniture scores.

When I moved to Boston, I started off in an airy, empty apartment. The wood floors added to the echo effect, and I wanted to furnish—fast! I wandered into an antique store a few blocks down the street from my apartment. It was so full, the furniture pieces were stacked one on top of another. Tables were perched precariously on couches, chairs hung over the side of armoires. It was mayhem.

who knew?

The most important item in your furnishing process? A tape measure. Loose measurements of your forearm on the wall are sure to bring about purchases that don't quite fit. Nightmare! Simply jot down proportions before you go so that you're sure everything will fit. And don't forget to throw the tape measure in your bag before you head out shopping.

But after only a few minutes, I'd found a beautiful dark wood desk, a tall wood dresser in the same dark stain, and two wooden chairs painted black that I could use for a number of things—desk, kitchen, stepstools. All of the items were in surprisingly good condition, and I asked if I could get a deal if I bought it all at once. Sure enough, the sweaty proprietor quickly busted out his calculator, *tap-tapped* away while scratching his head, and worked a little bargaining magic. The total price: $200 with delivery.

Unfinished

If you live by a college, you'll find an abundance of unfinished furniture stores. Generally, you can find some terrific deals on furniture here. The wooden bookshelves, tables, and desks can be solidly made and low-priced.

TIP: travel heavy

Stuck in the middle of an urban megalopolis, like Chicago, L.A., or New York, chances are the best furniture bargains are on the outskirts of town, or well past the borders. Instead of resigning yourself to paying more, find a friend who's also looking to furnish her apartment, rent a car, and make a road trip out of it. At worst, after getting a good deal on furniture, you'll break even on price and get a fun vacation out of the deal.

Last year, a group of friends in New York came up to Boston to buy a standing mirror at Crate & Barrel. Emily had seen the mirror in a Michigan store and loved it. Transporting it back to New York, however, would have been a nightmare from that distance. So she got on the phone, found it on sale in Boston, rounded up two friends, rented an SUV, and hit the road. They made a weekend of it, coming to town during St. Patrick's Day, hooking up for a grand fiesta with long-lost friends. The mirror, which they angled in the back of the car for the return trip, was simply the kicker.

At that point, you can finish them however you fancy: dark, light, painted lime green. The stores will offer to finish them for you, for a big addition to the price tag. Opt to do it yourself, lay down some newspaper, and paint away. I bought a wonderful collapsible five-level bookshelf unfinished for $80. I spent two hours painting it black and came away with a true bargain.

Ethnic

The Chinatown neighborhood in many cities is one of the best places to find low-priced housewares. While big items are scant—don't go looking for dressers, desks, or kitchen tables—the accessories are often low-priced and stylish. A mixing bowl, a colander, hanging lanterns. I love thin white crepe blinds, which complement without contrasting with most décor schemes. Any Chinese five and dime or large outpost stocks the blinds, and you can generally find them for under $20 each.

Thrift

A notch down from the average antiques shop, thrift stores can have a bad rep. But don't believe the hype. In a fancy neighborhood, or at a well-stocked store, you can find unbelievable prices on furniture. At one Salvation Army, I happened upon a cream and tan striped couch. It looked very Crate & Barrel, but the price was more along the lines of street curb: $50. It was a little mussed, so I bought some Woolite, scrubbed down the pillow covers, and called it a day. The end product was a sparkling couch that was worth at least a few hundred.

who knew?
The process of finishing furniture can add up to 30 percent of the price when you buy it completely done from the showroom. Do it yourself and save.

Big box bargains

There's a reason some call it Tar-jay, with ironic elitist inflection. The store is well stocked with some beautifully designed furniture and housewares, making a visit quite worthwhile. Modernist designers Philippe Starck, Michael Graves, Martha Stewart, and Jonathan Adler all contribute pieces from low-cost lines to the big box stores, Kmart, Target, and Wal-Mart.

Find lamps, kitchenwares, bathwares, and even furniture that has both moderate prices and sleek, unique designs.

Beware, though. Heading to one of the big stores hoping for a discount? Chances are that you'll end up buying much more than you had planned on, negating any bargain boon you score. Keep your eyes on the prize; start off with a list of what you've come for, and avoid impulse buys. Do you really need more mascara, a three-pack of Cheerios, and the new Backstreet Boys CD?

who knew?

Oftentimes, if you purchase many items at once, you'll get deals. Find a well-stocked store and come bearing a list of things you're in the market for. Bundle purchases, and bargains ensue.

QUALITY MARKERS IN FURNITURE

When investing in a piece of wood furniture, it's important to know that the range is far greater than dark to light, or fine grain to the kind likely to give you splinters. While honing in on bargains, keep an eye out for these signs of quality.

Handles and hardware: latches, handles, and hinges should be solid, well-designed, and firmly attached.

Inside: peek inside the piece of furniture. Is the wood in there polished and smooth or an afterthought? In a cabinet, are there liners?

Glides: in a dresser or cabinet, look for drawers that rest on wood glides. They should pull in and out smoothly, with no catch or stiffness.

Even legs: in tables, be sure that there's no wiggling, which is caused by legs of differing lengths. You shouldn't have to wedge folded paper under your furniture.

who knew?

One more reason to hold on to your student ID long after you've dropped the Freshman 15: stores like Pier I and Cost Plus give discounts to students at the beginning of each semester. Even if you move away from your college town, I've found they rarely ask about if you're a current student. Technicalities...

USE WHAT YOU'VE GOT

When furnishing your apartment, you could buy everything in ready-made sets of perfectly matched, discreetly distressed items at Restoration Hardware, or you could get creative with what you already have. Oftentimes, you have décor already in place—all you need to do is rearrange and think of it as such.

Books

Even if you don't have the complete gorgeously bound maroon volumes of the OED, your collection of books can be a decorating asset in your apartment. In a recent issue of *Martha Stewart Living*, there was a photo spread about Martha's daughter Alexis's cottage. Tucked into the side of a breakfast bar, in built-in bookshelves, Alexis had a collection of green hardcover books. Who knows what books they were. Does she read them? Are they actually even books? Who cares! They were a beautiful accessory in her home, neatly filed away.

Whether you keep them in orderly stacks on your coffee table or stashed in piles next to your pillow, your books not only become a window into your taste and aesthetic, they are also a wonderful decorating device. Organize by fiction/nonfiction. Organize by size. Organize chronologically. Organize by color. Organize by author name. But whatever you do, keep the spines aligned at the front of the shelves. Books toppling over each other turns a potentially good look into a messy disaster.

Mirrors

In a girl's apartment, a full-length mirror is a must. You can't go out without a full inspection to make sure there aren't any visible panty lines, terrible tugs, and unsightly hair poufs. But in other places in the apartment, substitute a mirror, in either a sleek black frame or a wooden one, for a piece of art. Over a mantelpiece or

TIP: wow woods

Find low-priced, well-designed furniture made out of these fine grades of wood, and jump on it:

Walnut (Cherry, Black)	Cherry
French Oak	Mahogany
Maple	Teak

couch, a mirror can even create the illusion of a larger room.

Pillows

Tossed on top of your bed, your pillows can either be an afterthought or an asset. Putting on a colorful silk pillowcase or stacking complementary colors one on top of another turns your bedroom into a veritable *ba-bam!*

FURNITURE TO SPLURGE ON AND FURNITURE TO SAVE ON

While it goes without saying that a girl wants the best of everything while furnishing her apartment, she must choose her purchases well. A fabulous couch, an entertainment center to die for, the perfect dresser, a four-poster bed. They may all seem like Must Buys, but the Urban Girl doesn't have the money for every little thing. Still, she need not resign herself to a room filled with dusty milk crates and overstuffed bean bags. The best thing about furnishing an apartment on a small budget is that it's easy to know what deserves the larger part of the furniture budget, and what can easily go low-end.

Reasonable measures

While you could easily drop thousands on a couch, why do so when you can find stylishly comparable items for half or a quarter of the price? Here's a list of reasonable amounts to spend on various items for your apartment:

Sofa: $200–$500 new, or much less if you can happen upon one at a thrift store. The best buys will be a futon sofa, which are also easily mobile and light. Beware! A non-futon sleeper sofa is where you end up paying the big bucks.

Mattress: $300 1-800-MATTRESS is a terrific resource, offering free delivery and well-informed staffers who know all the ins and outs and differences between firm, pillow-top, and rock solid. But like gym prices, the company discounts at lulls in the year. Avoid crunch times of September or June to purchase your mattress because many companies inflate prices then.

Dresser: $50–$200, depending on whether you buy it new or old. A used dresser is a much better buy than a poorly made new one. Buff the top and sides and call it a thrift score.

Kitchen table: $150–$300, depending on size and wood quality for a new table. Leaves are a key feature as they help to maximize precious space; they also provide an opportunity for extension, when you have guests coming over, or on Sunday mornings when you have the newspaper all spread out.

CD cases: $80–$200, depending on size. Avoid the fancy chrome affairs and go for classic wood staples, which fit more CDs anyway.

Bookshelves: $80, with unfinished shelves. Paint them any color or finish them yourself and avoid unnecessary fees.

Desk: $50–$200, with a desk you put together yourself. You can save bundles here.

Nightstand: $20–$100, depending on whether you can find one. Head to estate sales, which are listed in the Sunday paper. A deceased person's relatives are eager to unload the contents of their house. It can be a great place to find small pieces of furniture, which you can fit in your car or a cab.

Coffee table: $20–$50. Look online on message boards like Craigslist.org, where people hasty to get rid of their furnishings in order to move will slash prices in desperation.

TIP: from high to low, here's where to devote the dollars and cents

sofa

mattress

dresser or armoire

kitchen table

chairs

entertainment center

CD case

bookshelves

desk, side table

nightstand

coffee table

Worthy splurges

When furnishing her apartment, Dina, a twenty-five-year-old cookbook assistant and culinary student in New York, was operating with very little financial leverage. Like most Urban Girls, she had a small budget and specific ideas about what she liked. While she and her husband ended up getting most of their furniture as hand-me-downs from their

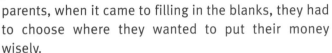

parents, when it came to filling in the blanks, they had to choose where they wanted to put their money wisely.

The ultimate splurge? Pillows. "A lot of our stuff is plain," Dina explains, "and the one thing we did is that we decided to splurge on pillows. So we have these incredible lush red pillows in the living room on the couch." The spread of pillows, six of which came to $800 at ABC Carpet & Home, all include special touches such as feathers, silk, and beads. "It brings the whole room together," she says. "I come into the living room and see them on the couch and they make me so happy."

Furnishing garnishes

As Dina did with her pillows, find your own signature splurge and turn it into a flair. A rug can have the same effect. In my previous apartment, I chose to decorate in a soothing, minimalist aesthetic. My color scheme was charcoal, black, and chocolate wood. To spice things up, I bought a black and white zebra-patterned rug, which added a finishing garnish to my room. Whether it's a wild rug or a lavish set of pillows, after you've decided on your decorating scheme and pared down all the wild colors, throw in your garnish to spice things up.

WILD WALLS

Once all of your furniture is squared away, the walls start calling. *Dress me up*, they purr. *Take me from boring bare to distinctly decorated.* A Warhol print would be nice, or perhaps a vintage rock concert poster. Here is an exciting opportunity for the Urban Girl to put the spotlight on her spunk and turn her talents into a piece she can showcase.

A few "outside of the box" wall décor ideas:

Paintings

Can't afford an original but pining for pieces you can hang? Take a piece of canvas and turn it into an *original first edition You*. Use a different wash of color on three square canvases and line them up side by side. Or use the same color on all three canvases and hang them on one wall with slivers of space in between them for a modernist touch. Another option is to take a favorite pattern on fabric (1960s bubbles, preppy stripes, happy faces), and use a staple gun to attach the fabric to the canvas. You can then hang it as an original work. Price? Under $50, all told.

Concert posters

Next time you're at a show and see cool-looking posters, rip them off the walls and paste them up on your own. Turn the posters into an inspiring collage above your desk.

who knew?

Read through all the catalogs and home décor magazines (from *Martha by Mail* to *Hold Everything* to *House & Garden*) to come up with your own useful ideas.

Little mirrors

Inspired by the television show *Trading Spaces*, Tracie took a trip to IKEA when she began to decorate her walls in her new apartment. She bought up a handful of little square mirrors, each individually framed for $1.99 apiece. They were a "gross green" color, which she then repainted hot pink. *Yowza*. Tracie hung them all aligned on her wall.

Multi-taskers

Sure, you could buy ten tables, four chairs, and little knickknacks that each have their own designated corner of the room. But when on a budget, a girl needs to be a little flexible. And with that comes convertible furniture. Just like when she buys a suit and wears the jacket and pants separately, an Urban Girl will do the same with her furniture, multi-tasking with the best of them.

Indoor/outdoor/everywhere

If a girl is lucky enough to have a patch of green to call her own, there's no need to invest in an entire set of lawn furniture, tiki torches, and mod plastic chairs as far as the eye can see. A good lightweight wicker table and chairs can transition from indoor to outdoor easily.

Stepstool steps up

Holed up in her tiny New York apartment, Sarah needed to get crafty with her furniture. So she bought a stepstool at IKEA for $10, painted it lime green, and carpeted it. She uses it as an extra chair when guests come over. You could also forgo the carpet and use it as a plant pedestal with droopy, leafy plants on the top and steps. When you need to reach into higher shelves, just remove the plants.

Storage

A trunk doesn't have to remind you of summer camp. A beautiful, aged piece can work either as a coffee table, a storage unit at the foot of your bed, or even a side table in the living room. Best of all, you can keep extra bedding, pictures, and valuables tucked inside.

free finds you can pick up on the street

t rash truly gets a bad rap: gross, dirty, smelly, unwanted. But litter is not the loser you might think it is. In fact, turn off the litter censor, turn those eyes down to the curb, and you'll find yourself awash in accessories, new furniture, new clothes. All for free!

From where does this bounty emerge? Some crazy people throw away awfully valuable loot. They've run out of time, they've run out of closet space, they've lost their mind. Whatever the reason, who cares? All the more for you. Consider the curb your very own Salvation Army, but even cheaper!

Think you might seem like a Depression Era hobo, hiking up your pants and diving into a dumpster head-first? No worries. Trash looting can be a classy, clean affair.

The first time I was introduced to the sport, I was walking toward Central Park on the Upper East Side. I was with Janet, one of my mother's closest friends from childhood, who then became my friend when I was in college. Mostly, we would go to plays together and fancy dinners at the latest trendy restaurant. But on this particular day, Janet introduced me to another form of culture: curbside pickup, rooting through trash.

On a late afternoon walk, a few blocks from the park, we passed a temple. I thought nothing of it, but Janet had stopped dead in her tracks, eyes asparkle. In front of the temple, on the curb, were stacks of garbage in open bags. Peeking out from the top were some beautifully bound leather books. "Wow, look at these," she marveled. "These are *gorgeous*!" She laughed briefly, acknowledging the impropriety of a wealthy fifty-something woman digging through garbage bags on the Upper East Side. And then she tucked them under her arm and we went on our way.

The world had opened up to me. Later that month, I was at my then-boyfriend's apartment when his roommate and his girlfriend wandered in, lugging a maroon velvet upholstered swivel chair. They grunted under the weight of it (apparently, it must have been quite heavy), and then they deposited it victoriously in the middle of the living room. "We found this on Amsterdam Ave," the roommate announced gleefully, grinning widely with hands on hips. They then took turns relaxing in the new/old piece of furniture. The price? Merely some sore arms and sweat—all it took in energy expended to bring the free furniture home.

Lisa is really familiar with the *sighing, lugging, dragging* entrance. Her boyfriend Michael is a "curbside rescuer," up there with the best of them. Walking around the city, he always sees things he wants to bring home and put in the apartment. And more often than not, he takes home the loot like a cat dragging in a dead mouse for dinner. Recently, while visiting Boston, Lisa passed a garbage can with a shiny standing red coat stand angled out of the top. "Michael would definitely want to bring that home," she laughed.

While sidewalks can yield serious scores for used furniture and loot, it's equally important to know when to walk on.

Here, a list of four rules you should follow, indicating the item is a *pass*:

1) It just rained
Soggy couches, wet wood, or drippy chairs aren't only heavier, they lose their luster, gain a less than snazzy smell, and seem forever damp. Walk on, sister.

2) The piece requires a financial infusion in order to save
Whether it's a couch that conspicuously lacks cushions, a chair without a leg, or a desk missing drawers, the item will need some pricey or timely TLC. Seriously weigh the boon-to-budget ratio. If you have to put in $30 to $50 to increase the value, you could most likely find a used item in better shape at a thrift store.

3) You're more than a mile from home without a car or beefy, willing friends
However compelling the curbside score, you've got to transport that fifty-pound hunka furniture back to your homestead. If you're likely to tear a ligament in the process, abandon ship, mate. That is, unless you can bat those eyelashes, coerce iron-pumping friends and family, or solicit the services of a large taxicab.

4) It doesn't go with your decorating scheme
Tiki may seem kitschy cool, but in your modernist pad the look will surely

clash. Free or not, avoid sacrificing your color scheme and overall aesthetic to save a buck. The Urban Girl has high standards that she must uphold.

SEASONS FOR CURBSIDE SHOPPING

Increasing your incidences of finding the best curbside loot is easy if you know when dumpster diving is in season. Just as fashion works on a seasonal clock, so do prime trash finds. May is the month when most students move out—hastily. Finals over, parents at the door, and summer sublets furnished, students find themselves with only a few hours to get rid of everything, from televisions to beds to lamps. And where better to dump them than just beyond the doorstep, on the curb? The departed's laziness can be a boon for cost-conscious shoppers, who could spend an afternoon and a boatload of cash shopping at the mall—or five minutes and zero dollars on similar stuff by taking a jaunt around town.

College towns are obviously the best place to go dumpster diving. Along with their notes and their expendable boyfriends (he was *so* junior year), students trash their furniture and clothes on a regular schedule: the semester system.

Sharon, an urban planner in Somerville, Massachusetts, was recently at a barbeque at a friend's apartment in Cambridge. She noticed hordes of U-Hauls blocking the streets and students packing them up. The light bulb sparkled on top of her head. *Score!* she thought, *Harvard students are leaving—and leaving lots of stuff.*

Sharon immediately gathered a few friends, one of whom has an SUV, and they prowled the streets that night. "We didn't even have to look that hard!" she said. "There was so much stuff." Sharon and her friends found sweaters with the tags still on them, designer dresses, and fancy shoes. "We filled garbage bags full of all the stuff we found," she said.

city chic • free finds you can pick up on the street

who knew?

In a college town at the end of a semester? You'll find the best stuff outside the international students' dorms. Long flights + good exchange rate + lots of spending + limited room in luggage = crazy castaways.

TRASH? THINK TREASURE

It would be easy to pass by many of the treasures on the street. You probably already have. They're the overlooked perks of living in a city.

But curbside castaways don't lose cache because someone else decided to trash them. Like cute abandoned puppies, all they need is a sponsor. You have to *bel-eeve*, sister; add in a dash of creativity, a hint of aspiration, and a healthy dose of faith. You have to get ready to get a little mussed, to take a Phillips head by the horns, to grab a hammer with conviction, and to lug until your arms feel like they're disembodied.

You earn it, baby. And your redone apartment, with your spruced up free loot, is your prize.

Room by room, here's what you can find on the street.

Kitchen
Table
Tablecloths are a marvelous thing. Find any kind of table on the street, and as long as it doesn't wobble too terribly (for example, the kind of wobble a wedged sheet of paper can't fix), you can throw a sheet over the table and have a terrific piece of furniture. Don't get hung up on gashes or curious stickiness.

Chairs
As long as there are four legs, a back, and a seat, a chair on the street is considered a score. Take two and paint them the

---

Even if you don't live in a college town or a student ghetto, the calendar year is marked by high and low Curb Shopping Seasons.

best months for curbside shopping:

August—September is a popular month for the start of leases, so start scouring the streets in the end of August in anticipation.

May—years after graduating, the start of summer still signals a time for changes. Leases end, people sublet, and the curbs fill up!

December—with presents and excess spending, December is a month of opulence and too much stuff. The key to this month is rescuing the curbside loot before it snows or freezes. A daily prowl can be fruitful.

January—all that December decadence requires a purge in January. Cash in.

same shade of lime green. Or go simple and slap on some black paint. If the chair is upholstered, even a rip or stain isn't significant enough to pass on the chair. You can always throw a sheet over it.

Don't do it

- **Platewear/glasswear/flatwear.** Walk on by. Really, you don't know where it's been. Unless you can have it industrially sanitized, pass on anything that will touch your mouth.
- **Food.** Need we even *explain?* This takes dumpster diving to new lows.

Bathroom
Hamper

A wicker hamper can be hosed down in and out. Then take a sheet, which you can cut and sew to fit inside as a little laundry bag. Sew a piece of elastic around the top edges so it hugs over the side of the basket, and voila! An $80 Pottery Barn-like accessory.

Wall units

A hanging cabinet, preferably with little compartments, can run as much as $150 at everywhere from Target to Crate & Barrel. Find one on the street, scrub it down, both inside and out, and paint it to match the walls of your bathroom.

Don't do it

- **Toothbrushes.** Scrub a dub dub? *Eew.*
- **Soap.** Lathering up with some random person's soap is a big NO.

Study
Lamps

Most likely, you won't be able to tell if it works until you get home and screw in a bulb, but as long as the walk isn't too far, there's no big loss if you turn the knob and *are* screwed.

Desks
The editors of *Bust* magazine in New York have a great DIY desk arrangement. They took a big slab of plywood and laid it flat over boxes filled with back issues of the magazine. Call it an "insta-desk." You could spend thousands on a drafting table, or you could get crafty like these savvy ladies. You'll have a free desk—and a great story.

Books
Like Janet's library find on the curb in front of the temple, recycling day is an especially fruitful day for curbside shopping for books or publications. Last month's magazine that you haven't yet read? Last year's *Zagats*?

Bedroom
Nightstand
This one is a popular curbside item. Chances are, take a walk and you'll see a nightstand or two. Why? Who knows. Perhaps there's a nationwide abundance of nightstands. No need though to get caught up in parsing out the "why;" dive right into the "where." What it means for you is that you can shop the curbs for the right one. Look for one that doesn't wobble, is the right height, and preferably has a drawer or shelves. Refinish or paint to make it your own.

Dresser
A tall wooden dresser on the curb is a goldmine. Since dressers can be so expensive, a free one on the street is worth the sore back and arms it requires to cart it back to the homestead. Make sure all the drawers work and there isn't any alarming smell that will seep into your special duds.

Closet accessories
Your closet floor is one big dust bunny with stacks of shoes. Clearly it's time to invest in some space savers. More space, more shoes! And where better to go shopping than on the curb? Keep your eyes peeled for shoe trees, which the occasional garbage bag will reveal.

Don't do it
- **Pillows.** Even with a pillow case, or even after a good wash, you do not want to lay your weary head down on some ratty pillow that's been parked on the curb, collecting car oil and people's loogies for weeks. Come on, pay $20 and get a new one.
- **Linen.** Similarly, climbing in a crisp bed of clean sheets can't be possible when who knows what went down on those puppies with their previous owner. Buy sheets new. No negotiations there.

Living Room
Entertainment system
Jane hasn't paid a cent for any of the electronic equipment in her living room. The TV, the VCR, the stereo. They were all gifts from the Secret Santa who leaves presents on the curb. Sure, the TV is circa 1957, but it still works! If you're the kind who only watches PBS (*sniff*), consider buying your box for free, too.

Couch
Couches have a great curb reputation. Because they're so bulky, people are less likely to transport them to be dropped off at the local Salvation Army. A potential score for you! Make friends with someone who has a truck. Be sure your couch has all its cushions and no overt springs. Remember, the idea is to find items that don't *look* like they just came off the curb. It must be a kitschy surprise for your dinner party guests.

Swivel chair
Failed dot com companies furnished many an apartment with cut-rate Aeron chairs and ergonomic gear. Head to neighborhoods with lofts and the like, or warehouses sure to be stocked in full chrome. These may yield the quality chairs, abandoned like so many dreams of dollar signs.

CD cases
A few slabs of wood, a shelf here or there; there's no reason to devote too much cash on CD cases when all that people will notice anyway is your impressive collection of old-school hip hop (that's right, original Afrika

Bambaataa and Grandmaster Flash). So keep your eyes peeled for one with enough room for your ever-growing stash of CDs.

Coffee table
There's really no need to get fancy with a coffee table. A standard table turns into a fashionable one when you stack beautiful books on top or refinish it. Simply look for one that suits your decorating scheme. Avoid Debbie Harry-inspired glass-top in your southwestern-themed, wood-focused apartment.

Don't do it
- **Rug**. If it's been on the street for weeks, your potential floorcovering could have been a potential litter box for street cats. And that is not an easy smell to remove. Still, if it's a find you can't pass up, stick your beak to the ground and make sure it won't infest your dainty apartment—and then get it professionally cleaned.

FIND YOUR CALLING—FOUND ART

Furniture is the obvious, in-your-face loot to snatch up from the curb. It sits there begging to be dragged off and rescued. Really, it's impossible to ignore.

But you're savvier and smarter than all that. You want the furniture—plus some. With your think-outside-the-box sensibility, you find lemons and make limonata; you take scratched, unusable vinyl and turn it into a wall display; you turn everything you touch into gold lamé, a piece of art.

Take a sled. Take a sign. Take anything, put it in a frame, or just bolt it to the wall. Stand back, assume the thoughtful position of stroking your chin, cock your head slightly to the side, and what do you have? ART. Who are you? A *creator*, an art-*eest*. If Warhol could make art out of the image of Campbell's Soup cans, you can make it out of the cans themselves.

Doug Fitch is an artist in New York who has turned found art into a successful craft. While walking around the city, he always looks for pieces that he can work with, souter together, paint, refashion, and turn into an entirely new piece of furniture. Recently commissioned to create a dresser for a customer, Doug spent two days trolling around several neighborhoods in Brooklyn. He picked up every dresser drawer he could find, assembling around fifteen to twenty. Some were severely weathered, but most were in fine shape. Doug took all the drawers and stacked them together side-by-side and three-to-four high, ending up with a monstrously long, arty bureau that takes up a wall in a loft. "It is elegant but practical, and very, very *nutty*," he explains.

Easy DIY found art
Globes
Lisa found an awesome antique globe on the street. She drilled a hole in the top, hung a hook, and strung it from the ceiling, where it spins. She can really be an armchair traveler. *Says: Woman of the World*.

Bicycle frames
If you're going for industrial, any scrap metal object will do. Bicycle frames, guns. Make sure you find a stud to bolt it to on the wall (and another stud to do the, err, bolting), otherwise your living room wall may crumble under the pressure. *Says: DIY Diva, not afraid to get her hands dirty.*

Antlers
In a funny, carnivore kind of way, a set of antlers in your living room could be hilarious. But not if your look is modernist. Remember to opt for simple unity rather than schizophrenia. *Says: Silly Sally.*

REFASHION FOUND FURNITURE
Whatever you find on the street is going to need at least a little spritz of disinfectant, perhaps a gruff sanding, and a few slaps of fresh paint. But in some instances, a bolt of fabric can perform a furniture rescue—or even create a nice touch to throw over some lovingly frayed hand-me-downs.

In a couch

Instead of reupholstering an entire couch, take a clean sheet, in solid or print, and place over the couch, folding down the sides and tucking under the arms to get a tight fit. When you wash your linens, throw this sheet in the laundry as well to keep it fresh and crisp.

On a chair

You can similarly rework a dilapidated armchair with a sheet. But in this case, finish off with a nice touch: tie the ends to the legs with ribbon bows.

Over a window

Bare windows are like undressed salads; they do nothing for you, but they can be transformed to a decidedly elegant affair with only a minor embellishment. Take a bolt of fabric, preferably a light linen, and hang as a swag over the top of a window. Keep a lot of extra fabric loose. Be sure to use colors in the same scheme as your walls.

With a pillow

Once you've "reupholstered" your couch with a sheet, you might want to toss on a few accents, perhaps a little pillow, for example. Find a bolt of fabric in something spicy, like red velvet. Cut into two equal pieces, stuff with anything soft, and sew it up. There you are, a fancy new couch!

INVENTIVENESS

A sheet can work wonders on upholstered furniture, transforming a dank couch into a one that looks new. But that's only one way you can use your inventiveness to refashion furniture, or even reuse something you might have been opting to trash. A crate? Shoot, why not make it shelves? Your old computer? Err...how about a coffee table??

Milk crates into IKEA shelving units

In the world of do-it-yourself decorating, the milk crate is the staple, the bread and butter, the proverbial white paint. Most starter apartments, whether they're the home of a graduate student or a publishing assistant, employ some sort of crate. But instead of stacking those splintery eye-sores and stashing them full of your Foucault collection in a conspicuous location (I studied *philosophy*!), think outside the, well, box. Find your milk crates on commando missions at night, behind grocery stores. When you get home, sand away to remove rough edges and paint them all black. Line one wall of your floor with them, two high. You can use these as book-shelves, CD cases, or magazine stands. Word to the wise: forgo the oft-standard cinderblock accessories to give the milk crates a little *lift* from the floor. That will negate any efforts you just made to disguise the milk crates and turn them into pseudo-IKEA shelves.

Vinyl records into coffee table accessories

Though the milk crate may be the staple, it is neither the *be all* nor the *end all* of furniture refashioning. In fact, it is merely a starting point. When surveying your lair, think of yourself as an inventor. Turn anything into something else. A terrific magazine exists called *ReadyMade*, from two Urban Girls in Northern California who have taken decorating inge-nuity to new levels. We salute them!

They came up with a wonderful idea about old scratched vinyl. Unless you man the wheels of steel at the local club and have use for scratchable records (*wicky-wicky*), the things are bound for the garbage bags. Ah ah....take those records, bend up the corners, and what do you have? An ashtray! Take a 45, gently cut down the circle, and what do you have? A coaster! Paste them up on the wall and what do you have? An arty display!

Old bottles into vases

Similarly, instead of recycling those wine bottles and sup-porting the guys on the corner who, in turn, pick them up the night before recycling, do some at-home recycling of your own. Soak the bottle in slightly soapy water overnight. That way, the label will peel off easily. Then take a few stems of dried flowers and place gently down the long vase. An old olive oil bottle or pretty balsamic vinegar bottle, with aged label, can also work, and depending on the label, you may just want to keep it on.

Cans into desk accessories

One of my favorite refashioning devices is to make use of old soup cans. Peel off every last shred of the label, wash thoroughly, and you have your very own chrome desk accessory. I use mine to keep pencils and pens in next to my computer.

final touches with flowers and plants

Y ou've put paint on the walls; you've arranged your lamps to emit the perfect off-the-wall lighting, all soft and ambient and ever-so-flattering; you've scoured the antique stores for pieces that are also furniture bargains; you've "rescued" a comfy and clean couch from the curb— thanks, neighbors! Now it's time for the decorating equivalent of the icing on the cake, the finishing spritz of perfume, the coy bat of the eyelash. Sure, your apartment is solid, but it only becomes something special—a *pad*—when you add the accent: flowers and plants.

FLOWERS' POWER

A fresh vase of sunflowers, a window box of bright pansies, a hanging fern. Sure, they're awfully pretty. But more than that, flowers are an inexpensive way to feel pampered, feminine, and decadent. Coming home after a day of off-the-hook phone ringing, crowded subway riding, and a bad date to top it all off, your apartment embraces you with a warm hug when you open the door and see a vase of fresh sunflowers. *Ahh.* Flowers do have power.

There's no room a little flora can't improve. A tiny vase in the bathroom of freshly picked wildflowers from your weekend getaway. A tall vase of lilies on your nightstand. A wide spread of pussy willows in the living room, resting on top of the mantle. A Chia Pet in the study. An aloe plant on top of the television. The opportunities to spread some life around your apartment are endless.

You don't need to turn your apartment into a jungle in order to breathe some life into it. Simply start off with a few stems and some potted palms to soothe all your senses.

YOUR PLANTS, YOUR BABIES

Having anything in your apartment that's living is a commitment. You'll need to water, trim, repot, serenade, massage. Damn, it's good to be a plant! Ignore or neglect and your sprightly décor will turn sour, offering a sad chiding "water me!" plea every time you peer over.

And there's nothing more depressing than seeing a plant slowly lose its life. I tried in vain to care for some flora during my college years. I'd start the semester all ambitious and eager, buying hanging flowering plants at a street fair every September. I'd proudly tote them home and find a bright spot, usually right in front of the window. At first, I'd have the best of intentions; I'd do the daily inspection to clear away leaf debris; I'd pat the soil to make sure it was the perfect level of moist. In short, I was a plant guru, and my minion was thriving.

And then, slowly but surely, over the course of a few months, my plants would lose a little luster, curl in on themselves, *visually weep*. In between racing from classes to the library to dinner to drinks and to bed, I'd sneak a peak at my slowly dying plants and wonder *Why? Duh*. I'd chosen high-maintenance plants during my high-maintenance lifestyle. They needed the daily care, and my hustle-bustle lifestyle wasn't exactly conducive to maintaining myself—much less some droopy plant.

So I quickly learned to buy better plants for my way of life. With more insightful purchases, I furnished my apartment with thick-skinned plants that could survive my occasional absence during a two-week-long vacation, Boston's blistering summer days, a smoky party, and getting completely drenched when I forgot to close the windows before a thunderstorm. *Sorry, guys.*

IS YOU LIFESTYLE MORE FAKE FLOWERS OR FERN?

You may find the idea of caring for plants an overwhelming prospect. Already, you barely find time for the weekly chat with Mom, the writing of the oh-so-necessary thank-you notes, the making of delicious dinners. And then you peek up from your doings and, oops, you forgot to water the old plant—again! It sits there drooping in the corner, wilting under your remorseful gaze. You bathe it in water, you purr at it affectionately, you smooch the dry leaves. But to no avail. Your plant is toast.

Molly, a part-time producer for a news magazine radio show, commutes between New York and Boston weekly. Upon coming home, she often finds the purple flowery plant on her front porch closed in on itself and parched. "It's like this," she demonstrates, sucking in her cheeks, shrugging her shoulders, scrunching her face. "But it has an unquenchable lust for life." Sure enough, she bathes it in water and it's back for Round 15, all happy and upright again.

Chances are, if you're constantly racing from work to appointment to weekend getaway, a full indoor greenhouse is going to be neglected—and any noble intentions for indoor lush greenery will be sacrificed to the trash chute. So do yourself a favor. Admit to yourself that daily waterings are going to be about as likely as actually scrubbing down your kitchen cabinets and opt for something a little more realistic but no less impressive.

As a general rule, the more high-maintenance you are, the lower maintenance your plants should be. But options in low-maintenance plants extend well past cacti and fake flowers. There's a plethora of flora options that require no more than an afterthought, a monthly watering (*when you remember*) and just the little glimmer of light your apartment has between the hours of 3 P.M. and 5 P.M.

TEST: do you lead a high-maintenance lifestyle?

If you answer "yes" to any of the below, you'll want to follow the clues in this chapter to find a plant that can weather your life storm.

- Do you find it difficult to find the time to shower every day?
- Can you currently smell your kitty's litter/kitchen trash/dog's hair?
- Do you have more than five saved messages in your voicemail—from last month?
- Have you recently forgotten your social security number/lost your wallet/misplaced your keys?
- Have you recently purchased more underwear as a way to put off doing your laundry?

If you answer "yes" to any of the above, you are not doomed to a plant-free zone. Simply read on....

PLANTS

Within the realm of decorative living, you basically have two options: plants or flowers. Cut flowers may provide a bright wash of energy, but plants are in for the long haul. They are a better option for the Urban Girl because caring for them well can be a worthwhile investment. Also, there are certain kinds of plants that actually have flowers and will provide the same breath of color.

When I finally came to my senses and invested in plants that would be able to live through my utter neglect, I found one that fast became a favorite: the Wandering Jew. It was a wispy hanging green plant that also had furry purple leaves. I liked having the color and the sprawl. Plus, I really liked the name. I felt like a Wandering Jew myself, constantly living out of trunks and avoiding large furniture purchases. How fitting that my plant thrived in the desert wasteland of my room! We could wander together.

Picking a plant

So you want a plant, but you're overwhelmed by the endless options (flowery, wispy, big, small, tall...*yikes*) at your local nursery. The first thing you'll need to figure out is what your apartment constraints are. This will help narrow down what kind of plant you can buy.

Option I: Your studio apartment has one window and it faces a brick wall.
Solution: You need a low-light plant.
Choices: Fern, Bamboo Palm, Chinese Evergreen

Option II: You live in Washington, D.C., and it's summer.
Solution: You need a high-humidity plant.
Choices: Boston Fern, African Violet, Nerve Plant, Peacock Plant, Spider Plant

Option III: You live in Palm Springs (*you lucky dog*) in the middle of a drought.
Solution: You need a plant that doesn't require much watering and that can take a little daytime baking.
Choices: Cacti, Weeping Fig, Aloe, Jade Plant, Burros Tail

Potting

Once you've selected the plant that is best suited to survive your personal crash course life, it's time to choose a pot. Simply stashing your new apartment companion in its flimsy black impromptu container on the windowsill and calling it a day negates this whole beautifying thing you're going for here. Take one more step, search out some pretty pots, and your plants will thank you.

The ideal pot will be either plastic or clay. Because clay pots tend to dry faster, if you're the type who forgets to water, go for the plastic variety. You'll either need a pot with holes at the bottom for drainage, or "rooting" at the bottom of a pot without holes. Before potting, stash a thin layer of bark at the bottom of the pot, then put in the soil and the plant. The rooting will help absorb the excess water. If you choose a pot with holes, be sure to place a dish under the pot to prevent minor flooding when you water.

Placement in the apartment

Even if your apartment is more Count Dracula than Sunny Delight, you can still make the most of what few wisps of daylight make their way through the cracks.

Go South

Generally, a south-facing window provides the best light for plants, while North facers are the darkest. (East and west windows typically provide the same amount of light, though western windows can be at a much higher temperature.)

Take a breather

Just like you crave showing some skin in summer, getting outside and frolicking, your friendly flora want some of the same action. Stash your houseplant on the stoop during the summer. Leave for a few hours—or a few days, if you trust your neighbors—and see how it fares. Does it perk up? Does it wilt? Respond accordingly.

Take a spin

If you leave your plant firmly situated in one spot, one side is going to get more lighting love than another. You may even notice the plant tilting—reaching, *creeping*—toward the window. Take it as a sign, o perceptive one, and turn the plant to spread the love to the other side. Turn plants every other week.

Watering

Though you may think that more water equals more love, in fact, drenching your plant with the aqua affection can make it rot. The best way to tell if it's watering time is the obvious one: pat the top of the soil. If it's cracked and dry, it's time to fill up the old watering can. You can also stick your finger or a match in the soil to see how far down the moisture spreads. In perfect conditions, it should be slightly moist at least an inch down. If the time is right to add some water, go gentle on the temperature. Plants tend to respond well to lukewarm water. Warm smothers and cold shocks.

Temperature

Hardy though your plants may be, stashing them in the window during a heat spell isn't likely to do wonders for the leaves' luster. If you're feeling a little wilted, chances are that your plant is, too.

Most plants thrive in daytime temperatures between 65 and 75 degrees. If you live in the desert, or your city is mid-heat spell, as your plant bakes, you'll need to take care of it in other ways to counteract the temperature shift.

Water. Water more frequently. Spritz with a fine mist in the morning.

Light. As your plant bakes, it will need more sun as well. Don't remove from a ledge.

Fertilize. Feed with fertilizer as well as water to ensure healthy growth.

Light

While south-facing may be best, sometimes a girl just doesn't have the optimal space and light conditions to create the perfect indoor greenhouse. When in doubt, she can get a little creative with her light sources.

- A track light from the ceiling, generally used for casting the perfect light on a work of art, also works well for flowering plants.
- Fluorescent light is used for flowers in many indoor greenhouses. But incandescent bulbs with wattage of 150 to 200 can also be used for low-light plants.

Maintenance

Consider your plant a baby, your wee one, the Urban Girl in training. Just like you, it needs its hair trimmed, its toenails clipped, a little exercise, a turn around the block.

Ideally, your baby will grow, add a few inches, outgrow its pot (*err, crib*). But you've got to help it along, use those nurturing feminine instincts.

Your baby grows up

If you notice your baby shedding/losing leaves, it may be because it's going through a growth spurt. Transfer to a larger pot, where it can lay down real roots.

Your baby needs some beautifying

Even if you opt for a low-maintenance plant, that doesn't mean you're completely off the hook. You still need to perform the perfunctory tasks to make your plant both pretty and healthy. Regularly snip off brown leaf tips with manicure scissors. Massage and loosen the top layer of soil. And remove all fallen debris from the pot. Out with the old, in with the new, so that your plant can get bigger and better.

who knew?

The spring and summer months, when daylight hours are extended, make plants hungrier. Summer is an active growth time.

Color me bad

Plants can communicate. Herewith, a translation guide:

Sign	Translation
Yellow	*Show me some light* or *I'm drowning*
Brown	*I'm thirsty*

Droopy	*I'm drowning*
Heavy shedding	*Water, please*
Black	*I'm dying here. Put me out of my misery*

Rescuing

So you've tried your hardest, you've purchased the plant voted Most Likely to Succeed. You've watered and whispered sweet nothings in your plant's direction. You've played a little Yo-Yo Ma occasionally to inspire the flora to be all that it can be. You've pinched and massaged, fed only the finest fertilizer, watered with lukewarm bottled Evian. But to no avail. The plant has a death wish, and it looks as if nothing, *nothing*, you do can interfere with its path to the trash.

Before signing off and saying the last rights for Flora the Fern, there are a few last-ditch efforts.

- **Repot:** try one last time to transfer to a bigger pot, starting out with fresh soil and fertilizer.
- **Mist** every morning for a week. Take a spray bottle and mist the leaves slightly.
- **Rake:** clear away all but only the fresh green leaves. That is, if there are any left.

THIS BUD'S FOR ME

Plants may be the best buy for the flora-loving Urban Girl. But sometimes, a girl just craves a tall vase of freshly cut flowers. In an engrossing essay, author Meghan Daum (*My Misspent Youth*) chronicled her financial travails as a young freelance writer in New York City. While she worked all hours plugging away at the keyboard, Daum managed to spend an astonishing amount of money, even while living frugally. Her poison of choice? Freshly cut flowers.

Flowers provide a touch of pampering. On bad days, pick them up for yourself. With a big work deadline looming, they inspire. After you've tackled a tough

who knew?

Pinching the end of a plant's new growth can encourage it to send out more buds. *Tickle, tickle.*

task, they work well as a reward. And as splurges go, they're a dramatically frugal one, especially if you buy your snapdragons and orchids wisely.

Here are a few options to get the same colorful lift without depleting too much of your funds.

Greenmarket—at the local farmers' market, you can pick up more than just plump organic tomatoes and thick brown whole grain breads. Many times, you can find flowers and plants there as well. Go late in the day, an hour before closing, and vendors are likely to slash prices.

Supermarket—the bigger the store, the cheaper the flowers; that's the general rule. You may not like to buy your produce at Safeway or Stop & Shop, but who says you can't find cheap carnations there? Big-box supermarkets have much better buys for flowers and plants than small corner shops.

Side of the road—make sure it's not someone's yard, or perhaps the endangered state flower. If all's clear, pick away, as close to the root as possible. Price? Free, i.e., the best buy possible. Some flowers just beg to be picked.

Everlasting

Fresh flowers may be the best, but the alternative isn't cheesy fake ones with the same vibe as plastic covered La-Z-Boys. Try dried flowers. First of all, the drying process in and of itself is decorative. Take a shiny red ribbon and tie off a bunch of flowers. Pin them to the wall, or tie it off on your blinds, over the window. Watch the water drain but the color remain. Once they're dry and crisp, you can take them down and place them in a vase. Or you may have become enamored with your new décor, so just leave the dried bunch up there.

who knew?

Still dead? Instead of trashing completely, if there's at least one useable twig, take a leaf and start fresh. This works best on aloe plants, where you can just slice off a fat leaf and pass it along to your friends.

Buying flowers at prime time

If you're buying flowers for yourself rather than to give as a gift, buy buds that are slightly closed so that you can see them open as well as

close. The life of your purchase will be much longer. That means they have been cut in the morning and full bloom is still to come. *Can't wait!*

The perfect time to buy a rose is when the bud is firm and slightly cracking, indicating that it's just about to flower. Squeeze the bud between your thumb and index finger. If it is soft and mushy, don't buy it, but if it is fresh and firm, it's perfect.

Making the flowers last

Day one with your freshly cut flowers is pure bliss. You wake up, open your peepers, and see the bright flush of color. You stick your beak in the center, getting pollen dust on your nose and inhale deeply. *Ahh.* But by day three, the flowers are curiously limp, hanging over the side of the vase. They are surrounded by a bed of dead petals. What happened?

To make your flowers last the longest, you can take some easy maintenance measures. And the payoff can add an extra week or two to your fresh bloom.

Right when you get home, cut off the bottoms of the stems. Cut the stem bottoms at a diagonal line ½ inch from the bottom with a sharp pair of scissors. Do your snipping under running water so the stems are exposed to the least amount of air. At the same time, take off any leaves that will be submerged.

Prepare your water. Fill your vase with lukewarm, but not cold, water. Add a teaspoon of sugar or a special mix the florist provides to feed the plant.

Keep the water fresh. Every morning, add a few ice cubes to the vase to keep the flowers cool and fresh.

When flowers start to wilt, make things right. Each day, you should be removing all dead stems and clearing the water of any debris.

Freshen up. Every three to four days, remove the flowers from the vase, recut the stems, again at a diagonal, and refill the vase with fresh water and sugar. If you've removed many stems, place the arrangement in a smaller vase to avoid drooping over the edge.

Hardy flowers

Whether your freshly cut flowers wilt straight away or stay sprightly for the long haul depends less on the color of your thumb (green or brown?) than on your ability to care for your recent purchase. But there are also some that just generally last longer than others.

These flowers are proven to last the long haul, at least one to two weeks, getting you more for your money. (FYI: Flowers from bulbs generally have a shorter shelf life.)

- Peruvian Lilies
- Orchids
- Gladiolas
- Sunflowers
- Hawaiian Ginger
- Protea
- Carnations

Other options

Lavender

Place the purple ends of the sweet-smelling herb from Provence in small bowls, which you can leave around your apartment. The fragrance will pervade the air and provide a nice swath of color. You can also stuff a handkerchief with lavender, tie it off, and stash it in your dresser drawers.

Bamboo shoots

Take the long spindly stems and place in a narrow vase with rocks at the bottom. Also, try carving round holes in a smoothed-out log at equal distances and standing the shoots straight up. Place in your windowsills to provide a green outlook on things.

Herbs

When growing plants, why not opt for something you can get some use out of? Try a planter of basil or thyme. Next time you're whipping up an Italian feast, tear off a few basil leaves instead of buying them at the grocery store.

who knew?

The best lighting for flowers is indirect, filtered light, rather than straight-on window glare. Place behind a slightly open shade, far from a window, and you won't bake your buds.

Pussy willows

In every apartment I've lived in, I always place a vase of pussy willows on the mantelpiece or dresser (if there isn't a fireplace). The long wooden stems and the little furry bulbs coming off are extremely low-maintenance, since they're dry and inexpensive to start with. And they provide a nice Zen touch.

Potted flowers

Instead of spending $1.50 a stem on sunflowers for the kitchen table, buy a potted sunflower; it presumably will last much longer while providing the same cheer.

BODY

section two

chapter five

toning down your fitness budget

it can get a little disheartening. Your wealthy friends swap notes about new moves their trainers taught them. You read interviews about how this or that millionaire lost a bazillion pounds. How? "Pilates!" they exclaim, as if it were a magic fitness potion.

Pa-what?

In the end, you mutter in defeat. *Yeah, yeah, I too could look like that if I had oodles of cash and time to devote to my body.* Seventy dollars a session for personal trainers; $200 initiation fee for the gym; $80 monthly dues to fight your way onto a sweaty, sticky StairMaster; $80 for another pair of shoes; $100 or so to drop in sporting gear, from sports bras to floppy shorts to the best pair of gym socks. Who knew that toning up would do such a number on your finances? In the process of losing weight, you can drop far more dollars than pounds—and the only thing slimming down is your wallet.

Well, stop morosely drooling over Janet Jackson's jaggedly cut abs and Madonna's ripped arms while feeding yourself fro-yo all weepy-like (*at least it's nonfat!*). Look at the female Adonises as simply inspiration; a goal to set for yourself; the finish line. Minus the paralyzed Botox-induced pallor; the trainer-inspired kickin' body; and the three hours a day to devote to your muscle tone, you can still rock it.

The stars may pay trainers to sculpt their bodies, attend to their limbs, and motivate them when they're dragging. But you just need to be a *leeetle* more resourceful. And it is possible.

Urban Girls are pumped up with more motivation than money, more inspiration to perspire than cash flow. Forget the personal trainers, the elite spa gyms, and the Yohji Yamamoto trainers. Who needs 'em?

CHEAP METHODS

Now that you're making your own money, it's time to choose the right sports. Skiing may be super fun—and you may have *finally* worked your way from pie-wedging to parallel—but it's not exactly a cost-conscious way to stay in shape. The $500 a weekend you can spend on lift tickets, hot chocolate, and ski gear could cover the annual dues to your local YMCA.

Below are some methods to stay in shape that will also tone down your fitness budget. As with anything, the prices vary. You could opt for super-fancy kicks, or you could scrounge for shoes from the clearance rack at Nike's factory outlets; you can attend a gym where they'll brush your poodle's teeth while you work out, or you can sweat *with* the oldies at the YMCA.

who knew?

Traveling and hoping to find the local pool? Log on to www.swimmersguide.com.

Running

Burn: 600 to 700 calories an hour

Running is one of the most frugal forms of exercise. All you need are a pair of shoes, a sports bra, and a path. Start the races.

I originally started running by sheer necessity—I was short on time and money. Senior year in college, I often found myself with thirty minutes to spare and a muscular itch in my legs. I needed to get out and move before heading off to another happy hour. But half an hour clearly wasn't enough time to go to the campus gym. So I'd throw on some shorts and run a couple of miles in Riverside Park.

It wasn't long before running became a fixture in my life, my favorite form of fitness. I became intimately familiar with portions of the path where the bricks spiked up and I needed to watch my step. I recognized fellow frequent runners and started to nod at them as we passed each other; but best of all, I replayed conversations in my head, thought through paper topics, and daydreamed about the latest cute boy from the library.

As for the fitness portion, sure, I liked it all right; my quads got firm and tight; my muscles responded well. But the bottom line was that running just worked for my lifestyle. And that was compelling enough to make me continue.

Wherever I moved after graduation, as I crisscrossed the country, running became a wonderful way to ground myself. It was a constant in my ever-changing life. I knew I could always just throw some sneakers in my bag and continue to get in my thirty minutes three to four times a week, as fitness experts recommend.

When I took my lowest salary ever, at an alternative weekly newspaper in Boston, there was no way that I could afford anything beyond a pair of shoes once a year. So while I took on extra freelance writing assignments, I decided to train for a marathon during nights and weekends. In the process, I fell into a community of runners around the city, I had plenty of therapeutic alone time, and I became the strongest I've ever been in my life.

What it costs: The expenses for running can be as high as you permit or as low as you'd like. Serious runners stock up on special foods like Gu packets, special high-performance shoes, special mesh tank tops, and souped-up padded socks.

But the truth is, normal duds will do just as well. Bananas and grape nuts pack in protein and fiber; a simple well-padded running shoe supports just as well as the fancy versions; "wife beaters" were my tank of choice ("wicking" moisture away is overrated); and any old sports sock will do as long as it doesn't have holes.

Experts recommend replacing your running shoes every four hundred to five hundred miles or after sixty-six hours of pavement pounding. "If you have a shoe you really like, go buy the same exact pair," advised Julie Cederborg, a former fitness editor at *Health*, who was also a marathoner. "On short runs, start off with the new ones, and keep a few pairs on rotation."

When I go to the gym, I use old cross-trainers rather than my running shoes, so that I don't wear them down. Invest in a solid pair of running shoes at a factory outlet like New Balance or Saucony. You can find a suitable pair of running shoes for $60 to $80, especially if you don't mind the occasional blinding fluorescent stripe on your shoes. Remember, style is not the number one objective here. You'll need three or four pair of running shorts, which you can wear a few times before washing if you do laundry bi-weekly.

As for other gear, all you'll need is a good tank top and a thin fleece, depending on your climate. I got a good fleece overshirt in the kid's department of Patagonia for under $40 several years ago that's lasted me through years of snowy runs, summer mountain runs, and courses through the urban jungle.

Walking

Burn: about 250 calories an hour, depending on pace

Everyone says that walking is the best form of exercise. The blood gets pumping, your heart rate rises, your leg muscles strengthen. That may be true, but there's another boon as well: walking is friendly on the wallet.

For Tracie, a twenty-three-year-old magazine writer, walking is her primary form of fitness. And that's for a few reasons. When finding an apartment, the one in her budget was about a half a mile from the closest subway stop in Brooklyn. *So long!* she sighed.

At first it seemed like such a drag to have to walk half a mile to the closest subway stop, and it would also unfortunately limit the kind of shoes she would be able to wear—*buh-bye high heels, hellooo fun sneakers*. But the commute from her house to the subway stop has turned out to be a blessing in disguise, a form of fitness. "I walk a couple miles a day," she says, "and that's just getting around."

You might not think that walking to and from various appointments does much for one's physique, but you'll be surprised by the results. When I was living in Washington, D.C., my commute from where I was living just north of Adams Morgan in Mount Pleasant down to 23rd Street was an unwieldy one. I could walk to the Metro (five minutes), transfer twice (twenty minutes), and then walk to work (another ten minutes), for a total of thirty-five minutes. Or

I could simply walk down there in about twenty-five minutes. I took to speed-walking, throwing on headphones and searching out cute shoes that worked well for clocking what turned out to be a brisk hour of exercise a day. And you know what? My days of walking in D.C. also happened to be when I dropped two dress sizes. You do the math.

Cathy, a newspaper editor in Boston, walks to work every day, from Brighton to the Fenway, a distance of a few miles. It helps her blow off steam and stay in shape.

At the end of a day under the fluorescent lights of her office, the walk is welcome. "It keeps me sane," she says. And in shape.

If you plan on walking but are looking for a little more *oomph*, you can supplement the simple one-foot-in-front-of-another affair. Try combining walking with another form of strength training. To attend to that rear end, flex your butt muscles while you walk; opposite leg/opposite cheek, and one, and two, and one, and two.

Take some hand weights and pump while you walk. Or, take a shoulder bag and carry it in one arm and then the other. It can actually work just as well as hand weights, when you consider the weights that add up from all of your books, magazines, makeup, and change. On a good day, you might have five to ten pounds you're lugging around in there.

What it costs: Walking, like running, is one of the cheapest ways to stay in shape. But walking is even friendlier on the finances than running. That's because it isn't as important to have top-notch shoes, since the impact on your body is less severe, minus all the bouncing up and down on pavement. Also, the gear isn't as important. Without the incessant jiggling, sports bras aren't a must. And sporty mesh tanks, well, need we even say more? Really, walking saves you money. There's no need for public transportation. Plus, if you opt to walk every day rather than hit a gym, you can avoid the expenses of monthly dues.

Swimming

Burn: 500 to 600 calories an hour

Depending on where you go, swimming can be a pricey endeavor. In big cities, it's often the case that the only gyms with pools tend to come with extremely high price tags. The pools are small, the lanes are often filled, and before you know it, you've been punched in the face by your lane-mate's aggressive freestyle stroke. *Thwap!* No thanks. But you just need to look a little harder. Instead of resigning yourself to finding a new way of staying in shape, or shelling out oodles to get access to the local lanes, think outside the Olympic-sized box.

Local colleges often have workable pools with public access during off-hours, or off-season.

The YMCA, YWCA, or Jewish Community Centers often have pools, and membership can be quite inexpensive.

Many cities have municipal pools with annual dues. It's a low-frill affair, so be sure to bring flip-flops and your own shampoo.

What it costs: Beyond the price of dues to get a spot in the pool, the expenses for swimming are really rather low. You'll need to invest in a good, solid lap-swimming bathing suit, which can range from $40 to $80, depending on the make and strength of the fabric. A good pair of goggles with strong elastic band and a swimming cap won't run you more than $10 to $15 at a local sporting goods store. And there it is, your entire fitness budget. Oops, one last thing: don't forget to invest in a trusty regular bikini wax so as not to scare the little kids.

Pilates at home

Burn: between 300 and 400 calories per hour

For months, I'd been hearing about the sport like it was some sort of manna for the physique. *Pilates*, people would murmur with a faraway look in their eye, *I've never been in better shape*. It sounded like gift from the heavens. Once I learned how to pronounce Pilates (Pah-lah-tees), a set of exercises developed for dancers to strengthen the core of the body, I realized that a gym I'd just joined was offering classes. Why not try it?

Just by chance, I fell in with a wonderful young teacher named Jessica, and I soon became one of the inner circle of attendees. We'd arrive early, get the good mats, and claim spots in prime territory in the room, right under the heating vents. Within months of going either once or twice a week, I developed definition in my stomach muscles, something I'd never had before. But when I moved apartments, and had to leave my beloved class, I didn't know what I was going to do. Pilates minus Jessica didn't seem like a worthy enterprise.

I'd tried doing the exercises by myself at home one day when I was snowed in and unable to attend class. It was possible, but I just needed a little direction. So I brought a tape recorder into class and recorded Jessica's one-hour session. I bought a book and started teaching the exercises to myself. Now, when I have guests in town and can't duck out for class, or when I have only a short amount of time in between appointments, I'll do a series of exercises that don't require anything at all. No weights, no hardwood, no mats, no paraphernalia. I'll just whip out a few of my Pilates moves, making sure to stretch long and hard both before and after.

Try it yourself; it worked wonderfully for me. Find a teacher you like, make sure she's OK with your taping the class for your own home use, and bring the class home with you. Just make sure your teacher doesn't have an annoying voice or a head cold. After listening to a raspy cough time and time again, you may just want to pick up and take kickboxing instead in frustration.

the pilates 10

Pilates is a series of exercises built around integrity of motion. It's not about what you do, but how you do it. There are ten fundamental exercises that make up the basics of Pilates. Invest in a book like Eleanor McKenzie's *The Joseph H. Pilates Method At Home: A Balance, Shape, Strength, and Fitness Program.* After you take a few classes and get a book, you can continue the exercises at home for free. All you need to do is follow the Basic 10. They are:

1. Hundreds
2. Roll up
3. Leg circles
4. Rolling like a ball
5. Stomach series
   - Single leg stretch
   - Double leg stretch
   - Scissors
   - Leg drop
   - Shoulder cross
6. Spine stretch
7. Corkscrew
8. Saw
9. Side kick
10. Seal

What it costs: Around $15 to $20 for the mat. A few bucks for the cassette tape. And some loose-fitting pants.

At-home videos

I was raised by two parents in San Francisco who actually attend "yoga camp," a retreat with other '60s-era radicals in Montana, where adults stretch by day and perform skits by night. Needless to say, I resisted the *omm* in my life until rather recently. It felt like cheesy, New Age, hot-tubbin' lovin' to me.

But once I started getting in on the triangle pose action, I realized the beauty of the ancient practice. I started regularly attending a class with a stern yet spiritual teacher who treated us like we were on the semester system: attendance was key; progress was paramount; and missing a session was frowned upon. I fell in love with the feeling of deep stretches, blood thumping into new places in my body, and pain being merely a transitional state. But the weekly class, at $18 a session, was a luxury I could only enjoy by scrimping and saving in other places. So I bought a yoga mat and a video and tried doing it at home. That lasted for about a month before I found myself talking back to the irritating professor on the tape. Had I bought the wrong video?

Apparently. Buying the right exercise video is integral to sticking to your routine. You have to make it easy on yourself. Here's what to look for in your video:

No false promises
Beware the toned, spandex-clad, orange-skinned gym bunny who promises X number of pounds lost in X-minus-one days. The video will only be as successful as you are at following it.

Avoid the She-Woman or He-Man
You're not looking for heroics or a circus act. If the instructor moves too quickly or uses words like "pump it up," chances are you'll be diving for the eject button before you even break a sweat.

Buy now, buy more later
Watch out for a video that requires a slew of bells, hoops, and whistles. You shouldn't need to invest in anything other than the video itself. Like recipes off of one brand's cereal box that require all other ingredients to be of that brand, a bad video will push you to purchase bogus paraphernalia.

Take it down a notch
Just like in real life, it's important to find an instructor that balances firm direction and calm support. A yoga instructor with a harried, shrill, or panicky, breathless tone practically ensures you'll lose interest fast. Remember: *omm*.

ANYWHERE EXERCISES

It seems the Urban Girl is always on the go. Whether it's running out the door to meet friends for a picnic in the park or trying to catch the last showing of the new Wes Anderson flick, her schedule is as crammed as her closet. But staying in shape isn't something she likes to sacrifice in the process of maintaining her go-go schedule. Instead, she picks up on free, easy exercises she can squeeze into her schedule anywhere, from hotel rooms to her bedroom floor.

Jumping rope

You played in grade school, some of you even competed. But this is one sport that loses its cache pretty much the same time that girls graduate from *Seventeen* to *Cosmo*. But don't diss too fast; jumping rope has seen a resurgence around the country; people are fighting to have the hippity-hoppety activity taken seriously as a sport.

And why not? You buy one piece of gadgetry, or substitute a piece of rope, and there you have your entire fitness budget. Fast rope-jumping for short periods of time burns more calories; slow rope-jumping for a longer period of time promotes fat burning and strengthening of the limbs. Best of all, jumping rope is a wonderful solution for fitness-fiending travelers. Simply throw a jump rope in your bag and get started. Hotel rooms, guest bedrooms, anywhere. All you need is a few feet in front and behind you so as not to lash someone with that whip of yours.

Running stairs

Even without a stadium, you can find a good stairwell to tackle. Stuck without my running shoes at my parents' house in San Francisco for a week, I had to come up with some way to move. Luckily, the house is a typical San Francisco stair-filled affair. You have to walk up two flights simply to get to the front door, you must climb another flight to get to the bedrooms, and yet another to my parents' bedroom. So I got started, pumping my arms, walking up and then down backward. Within minutes, my heart rate was racing. The next day, my calves were tight, a pleasurable result of having worked them strenuously the day before.

If you're in the vicinity of a series of stairs outside, running up and down works well; it strengthens the quads in your legs and boosts aerobic capacity.

Elevator exercises

Next time you take the elevator, don't just stand there. You may not be getting the benefits from taking the stairs, but you can still make the most of your transport. Try some of these exercises. Just make sure you're alone!

Squats. Bend your knees to a 90 degree angle and pretend you've popped a squat in a chair. "Sit" until you reach your desired floor.

Pushups. Stand a foot back from the wall and have your back to the elevator door. Place your hands shoulder-width apart at shoulder height. With your elbows close to your body, start your vertical pushups, slowly and with integrity of motion.

Leg stretches. If there is an arm rail (and you're not wearing a skirt) place your leg on the rail and start a deep stretch.

Extreme chores

After a long day of painting your apartment, you realize that you have discovered muscles in your upper back and arms you didn't know even existed! Sure enough, flecked with paint and dizzy with the fumes, you've figured something out: chores can secretly provide exercise. Consider it multitasking bonus points.

Researchers around the country have long been studying the beneficial physical results that come with keeping house. In fact, things like gardening, sweeping, mowing the lawn, and washing the car are all boons for the heart and muscles.

Weight training

For many women, weight training is an intimidating affair. When I head to the gym, I have to force myself to go into the testosterone zone of vigorous grunting and sweaty benches. I feel ridiculous with my wee weights (*ten pounds is good enough for me, thank you very much*). And I don't really want to go back the next time, no matter how much I know it will help prevent osteoporosis thirty years down the line.

But Lisa, a twenty-six-year-old writer in Brooklyn, came to love pumping a little iron. In her college days, she got in the habit of using hand weights in her room every morning. She had a quick routine worked out that involved various stretches with weights, dancing around a bit, and muscle strengthening. For fifteen to twenty minutes every morning, she'd pick up the weights and do her routine. The result? "It was the best shape I've ever been in."

did you know that these activities burned this many calories?

Activity	Calories/minute (in a 120 pound woman)
Bowling	1.2
Getting your groove on at a club	2.9
Gardening	5.0
Walking	6.5

The U.S. Surgeon General recommends burning at least 150 calories a day. You can easily reach that number with thirty minutes of activity at some point in the day. But did you know that these daily tasks did the job? (In a 120 to 150 pound person)

Activity	Amount of time
Wash dishes	45 to 50 minutes (must be a lot of dishes)
Vacuum	25 to 30 minutes
Stack firewood	15 to 20 minutes

I keep two five-pound weights in my living room. Any time I have some spare time—whether it's during commercial breaks of *Real World*, or in between phone calls—I'll pick up the weights, do some curls, some over-the-head pumping, and some lunges.

A pair of five- or eight-pound weights will do the job well. At the least, they will get you started for the first couple of months until you are well on your way to being *Ah-nold*.

GYM MEMBERSHIP

All these things are fine and dandy when it's nice outside. They may round out a fitness routine. But sometimes, a girl just wants to join a gym and get into a nice routine. *StairMaster Monday, Ellipses Tuesday, Yoga Wednesday, StairMaster Thursday, etc.* But simply take a look at all of the breathless advertisements in the local paper to join a gym, and all of the price-changing promotions, and you'll quickly learn that prices rise and fall about as frequently as your weight does: i.e., every day.

The big secret is that **gyms negotiate.** Play hard-to-get and coy and watch the prices drop. A friend handed me a stack of guest passes for her gym, which I started visiting, pretending to be interested. It was much nicer than the YMCA that I'd been frequenting, which had a moldy smell about it. After taking the full tour and feigning hedging each time I visited (*I really like it, but I'm not sure. I'll have to come back tomorrow*), I started to really like it and flirt with the idea of joining. On the umpteenth sit-down with a membership salesperson bursting out of his uniform, I said I really wanted to join but was unable to because the price was simply too high for me. I started walking out the door. He called out to me as I was leaving and dragged me back. With a quick swipe, he slashed the price practically in half, making like it was our little secret. *Oops, I just told.*

Best time to join?

Like stores' sales, gym memberships fluctuate seasonally and monthly. Buy in at the right time, and you can score a great rate or have your initiation fee waived. When should you shoot for savings?

End of the month: By the end of the month, membership salespeople at gyms are staring down the sales figures. If they haven't hit the target, they may make a deal to hit projections.

Any major holiday: Gyms use any calendar opportunity to create an event out of special occasions.

Beginning of the year: Join the well-intentioned masses in January and head to the local gym, where they have a resolution that matches up with yours: sign up new members. Counterintuitively, the rise in demand is actually a boon for the consumer because they're likely to make a deal.

who knew?

One in five people between the ages of eighteen and thirty-four belong to a health club. If you're a member of the club, make sure you're getting the best rates.

TIP: some of most expensive sports and ways to get in on the action

Raised on downhill skiing, squash, and tennis, you want to continue to participate in the fun sports. But chances are that now that you're footing the bill, it's more of a stretch. Don't give up hope. Get in on the action, kind of:

Instead of	Try
Downhill skiing	Cross country
Squash	Handball in an outdoor court
Indoor tennis	Outdoor tennis
Golf	Putt-putt
Rock climbing	Hiking
Rowing crew	Canoeing
Yachting	Community boating

Beginning of the semester: If you live in a town with lots of students, gyms hope to attract coeds when they hit town. Walk in with a stack of books (I just forgot my ID!), ask for the student rate, and give it the old college try.

Clean up and get a discount

Just as you can wash dishes to pay a dinner bill when in dire straits, at some gyms you can swipe down sweaty machines and clean up a few hours a week to pay for your membership. Ask around to see if you can strike a deal and barter, old-school style.

who knew?

Gyms are competitive places—even when it comes to membership. Keep your old gym cards and tell them you're switching from your old gym to theirs (the facilities here are so much better!). They will often give further discounts if they think they're snatching you away from the competition.

chapter six

snip your hair care budget

"I have friends who
cut their hair themselves,
all jagged, and it looks
fantastic!"

—Antonio Prieto

haircuts are like oil changes. People will try to convince you to get on a regular schedule, or else! *Your car will fall apart, your sheen will shed, you'll be doomed, my friend. Doomed!*

The amount of time in between visits varies: every six weeks, every ten thousand miles, every three months. Whatever the doggedly imposed deadline to head to the pros for upkeep may be, it seems a little rigid. Haircuts are one area where one size definitely does not fit all. And getting you in for servicing eight times a year may be more advantageous for your salon's coiffeurs than your sleek coif.

Sure, you'll meet the girl (or maybe you are the girl) who responds, "Well, *I* for one *absolutely* need to go in every six weeks. My hair just starts looking like crap if I wait much longer."

But we're all familiar with the hair desperation. One morning you wake up, peer in the mirror, and see frizz-city, shaggy doo-doo up there. You reach for the trusty hair band to tie it up. But as soon as you've smoothed out all of the pesky hairs, you realize the truth: another day of ponytails will just not cut it. You decide you cannot take it One More Second. You call the salon in a tizzy, begging to be squeezed in on Saturday morning at 8:45. Brutal, but necessary.

The big secret of haircutting is that there is no need to keep heading back for maintenance on such a regular schedule. A good cut will last and have as many lives as your cat. As it grows out, you'll find your hair assuming new positions. If you get a good, long-lasting haircut, the every-six-weeks schedule will turn into ten weeks, which can even stretch into fourteen weeks, advises an expert at Vidal Sassoon.

SEARCHING FOR THE RIGHT SERVICE

The first step in paring down your haircutting budget is being honest with the person who cuts your hair.

Find someone you trust, who makes you feel comfortable, who talks you through the process.

Inform them of your history

Be sure to clue in your haircutter about what looks you've had in the past. What's worked and what's been a big bust? Are bangs a haunting memory from sixth grade? Does the Jennifer Aniston *Friends* 'do bring back cringe-filled memories?

Don't be nervous about being firm about your needs (i.e., "I used to be a six-week woman but I'm trying for something more long-term now").

Signs you should jump out of the chair: the person drops his/her shears in horror about some of your history, the haircutter interrupts you each sentence to air-kiss passing clientele.

Release Control

The best-case scenario with a hairstylist is to find someone you can trust completely, someone who oozes expertise, whose calm, cool demeanor says, "I know exactly what to do with you. Trust me."

At various points in my life, I've found haircutters who I don't even try to instruct. I dispensed with the glossy photos of Gwyneth, Reese, or Meg. I put them down, hop in the chair, and say, "I put myself in your hands, do your worst. I am yours."

Be clear if you've cheated

It's hard, but you won't fool anyone if you've been serviced by someone else. Your haircutter will inspect your locks and look, expectantly waiting for the confession of cheating. I always feel a little sheepish when I go to another person besides my main haircutter. I'm apologetic and embarrassed. But there's really no need. Be honest. Your hair is a palette that many artists can touch. While it may be best to have

TIP: responses that indicate you need to find a new hairdresser

- *Well, the only thing I can recommend is to chop it all off and get you a razor. Cool?*
- *It's every six weeks or nothin', sweetie. Suck it up.*
- *Well, you can wait a few months before coming back, but I'm warning you, it won't be pretty....*

one person attend to your cut—for consistency's sake—sometimes you have a one-shot deal at having your locks tended to by a salon superstar.

My friend Lisa, a documentary filmmaker in New York, had the chance to participate in a live video shoot/art project that involved having a designer cut her hair while she was standing on the flatbed of a truck driving through downtown New York. The result? A nightmare for her hair, but a success, art-wise. People stopped in the street, clapping, watching in awe. Post-project, Lisa just went back to her regular person and pleaded: *save me!* While monogamy may not be realistic, confession always does the trick. Find someone who won't chide, guilt-trip, or play hard-to-get when you come back with your tail between your legs.

CUTS THAT LAST

Once you find the right person, your trust will pay off big time. Most importantly, you can let your haircutter know about your financial constraints. You can tell him or her straight up that six weeks just won't do. That you're looking at more like ten, fourteen, or twenty, whatever it is. "Be clear if you need to maximize your haircuts," advises Patrick McGinley, the creative director of Boston's Vidal Sassoon. "Then I won't give you a cut with a six-week lifespan."

I've gone as long as five months in between haircuts. It was definitely a stretch, though, caused by equal measures of laziness, experimentation, financial crisis, and shifting priorities. Two hundred dollars for a haircut and color? *Puhleese*. I found much better ways to drop the cash: traveling, manicures, dinner out with a new boyfriend. My hair became a low priority.

The 5-Month Haircut Experiment

Here's how it went. In mid-August, I had my hair cut into a choppy, short, spiky blonde bob. In the morning, I'd throw in a healthy dose of Kiehl's Grooming Creme as it was drying and be out the door without thinking about it for more than a passing second.

By October, my hair had grown to just below my ears. I'd snap barrettes into it, haphazardly, or simply use headbands. Sometimes I'd comb out the natural curls and wear it sleek and straight.

By December, things were getting a little scary up there. But by that point, the hair was long enough to pull it back into a low, short ponytail at the back of my head. All the layers had grown out. And I was able to work that look for about a month, through the end of the year, before banging down the door of my salon in total and complete desperation. Help! The original cut wasn't cheap ($70) but going three times a year (every four months), rather than every six weeks made it worth my while.

Annual Hair Care Budget

Stretching out the time in between salon visits adds up—fast. Ditch the every six weeks rut and opt for longer spans. See how fast you save.

For a $50 cut, including tip

Interval	Annual Expense
Every six weeks	$425
Every eight weeks	$325
Every ten weeks	$250
Every fourteen weeks	$200
Every twenty weeks (ahem)	$150

To lengthen the amount of time in between visits, it pays to splurge for a quality cut. Pay more up front and go longer in between salon visits.

For a $100 cut, including tip

Every six weeks	$850
Every eight weeks	$650
Every ten weeks	$500
Every fourteen weeks	$400
Every twenty weeks (ahem)	$300

What to look for in a cut that will last

Sometimes, no matter how much research you do, it all comes down to trial and error. You figure out that shaggy is definitely not saucy on you; that straight makes you look like a Madonna casualty in her faux-British phase. But all hope is not lost, and there's no need to turn yourself over to fate in extending the longevity of your haircuts.

Layers

If your hair is long, opt for longer layers on the sides and in the back. They'll grow out nicely. Alternately, short layers will look dumpy initially and then grow out to look like you just stepped out of a trailer (and I don't mean movie trailer).

Length

It's sort of a no-brainer, but a short cut is always a good idea if cost is a concern. The cut can grow out and adopt several different personas as time passes.

Looks

A classic bob is always a nice bet for the budget-conscious girl. At first, a short bob looks sleek. But then it can grow into a chin-length bob, which naturally sweeps lower as time passes into shoulder length. The look makes the transition of time quite well.

THE BOTTOM LINE ON BANGS

For some, bangs are a bad idea. I'm one of those people. When I was young, an evil hairdresser convinced me that it would be cute. But my wavy hair immediately sprung to attention on my forehead, frizzing into a bouncy mop. I was a fashion disaster—and there was no saving me.

In order to leave the house every day, I was doomed to a pesky time-consuming fate: blowing out my bangs each morning for thirty minutes to get them paper-thin and straight. God forbid, it rained, and then I became the human water dog again as the humidity thwarted my A.M. efforts.

TIP: People who should never have bangs. Girls with:
- Curly hair
- Long foreheads
- High hairlines

Now, when I tell my trusty salonistas about the bangs fiasco, we laugh. And then they ask me who in god's name thought that bangs were a good idea for wavy-haired moi. There's no need to become a bangs casualty like I was back in the day. Just figure out if your hair type and facial specs will be hospitable to the look.

Bang-cutting techniques

When I first moved to Boston, I noticed a look all over the city, at rock clubs, at cafes, on the T, that was uniquely Boston. Girls with deep black hair and blunt-cut bangs. Most times, the bangs were cut quite short, more than halfway up the forehead. The line was severe but also cute. It was really cool, in a retro rockabilly sort of way.

But blunt-cut bangs are far from a low-maintenance look. Within weeks, they're creeping down your forehead, itching your eyes, flying up all over the place, wreaking hair havoc. You basically have a few-week window before the cool look grows into a scrappy mess.

If bangs are a must, simply learn how to trim them yourself.

Avoid the mistakes we've all made as preteens. Ambitious and trigger-happy in front of the mirror clutching scissors, you got creative, snipping just a *lee-tle* more, evening out the edges just a wee bit more. Until, *jeeezuhs*. Help!

First you need to get a grip

There is a right way and a wrong way to hold scissors. It's important to get a good grip; haphazardly throwing any old digit in the scissors loop could lead to a quivering disaster, zig-zaggy hairlines, and, subsequently, rivers of tears. What did I do?!?!

TIP: Cutting bangs in between

Ground rules
1) Cut when dry.
2) Style before snipping.
3) If you're trimming in between cuts, never take off more than an eighth of an inch at one time.
4) Don't tug. You'll take too much off.

Sooo. Get it right. Your thumb should go in the big hole, your ring finger in the other, and your index finger on top. Use whatever hand you write with. This placement should lead to a sure, steady snip.

Sheer action

Comb bangs straight down. Gather them in a well-angled triangle with the tip somewhere between the eyes. Cut straight across. The result, when you release the triangle of hair, will be a straight line. When in doubt, cut less than necessary. You can always take off more. But you can't go back once the hair has fallen on the floor.

who knew?

Vidal Sassoon offers complimentary bang trims in between cuts. You can just pop in any time to be serviced. *Hellooo, I'm back!* Ask your salon if they'll do the same.

COLORFUL EXPENSE

While haircuts can take a significant chomp out of your budget, coloring is where the real damage is done. With highlights hugging the $200 mark at some top salons and single color washes topping that—all for an element that requires serious, regular upkeep—consider coloring a black pit of expenses.

Confession: I'm addicted to highlights

I started putting blonde highlights in my hair junior year in high school. I was reluctant at first; my hair seemed good enough then. Why change anything?

My natural hair color is a dirty blonde that perks up when exposed to the sun. But the first time I walked out of the salon with my blonde hair sparkling, I was sold. *When should I come back?* And I was a slave to the salon. Within no more than two to three months, my darker blonde roots were showing and no matter how I scrubbed up or dotted on sexy perfume, I always felt unkempt. There's nothing worse than exposed roots to make a clean girl feel gross. I wasn't exactly going for Courtney Love's pre-glammed out, mottled look.

Beware. Coloring becomes addictive—a necessary evil, because once you start, you become a slave to tending your roots. So think twice about taking the plunge. It can be costly, addictive, and an ever-ending chore. That said, lighten up!

Choose your poison

Once you've decided to get a whiff of the color drug, it's important to choose the right one. Unless you're a goth or an art student, you'll want a color that complements your skin tone rather than clashes. Dark black hair with my fair skin would certainly say something—but not exactly the message I like to present. Think goth Angelina Jolie at the famous brother-smooching Golden Globe ceremony.

More importantly, beyond the image aspect, severe clashes may be cool-looking, but they will require costly upkeep. For example, when my roots start to show, blonde on dirty blonde is easier to pass off for an additional week than say, black on dirty blonde. If low cost is a key factor in deciding your hair color, there is one simple rule to follow: use complementary colors.

MAINTENANCE

Most of the challenge in trimming hair care costs lies in maintenance. The better you care for your coif, the longer you can hold out before heading back for another cut. In between those cuts and colors, especially if you're seeing how long you can go, you can do certain things to make your looks last.

Drop the shampoo daily habit

Washing your hair every day is actually self-defeating. Ever notice how on day three of your rugged camping trip, your hair looks hot? Or how after a day at the beach, all sandy and sticky, your hair does some cool flip you cannot recreate that night after a shower and an hour in front of the mirror? That's because it's dirty, and this is one time when dirty girls win. Your hair has natural oils that need time to travel down from the roots to the tips to moisturize and add volume.

That's why Vidal Sassoon's Patrick has always tried to convince his girlfriends to wait as long as they can. He's even begged and pleaded with them not to wash their hair every day. "I tell them, believe me, trust me; wait as long as you can. It will look great." Conserve shampoo, your haircut, and color by lathering up every other day or every third.

That can be tricky if you're a daily gym bunny. You need to shower off after yoga class or a session on the treadmill, but you're on your off day for shampooing. What to do? There's no need to forgo a shower. Simply go through the motions in the shower, pretend you're lathering, but just use your hands and water. And then, as you dry your hair, put on new products. You head's oils will act as a natural conditioner, moisturizing and maintaining the color for longer. Simply stop shampooing every day and you'll dramatically extend the life of your highlights or color.

who knew?

Girlfriends are good for many group tasks. Why not have a hair-coloring party? Get together with drinks (not too many if you want to leave laughing instead of crying) and supplies. Come away New Women with New 'Dos. Just follow the instructions...and go easy on the pouring.

Opt for the right poison

You want to do everything you can to care best for your hair, but is it really necessary to buy those $20 bottles of shampoo and conditioner for color-treated hair?

No way, say hair experts. You could even use a $3 bottle of baby shampoo. Color-safe hair products are mostly just extremely mild. When searching out the right products, simply look for something that's not harsh or acidic, which will oxidize your fine head of hair and strip away the color.

Go light on the ponytails

Ever notice that girls constantly tying their hair in ponytails often have wispy fuzz around the face and split ends on the crown of their head? That's because hair rips. If you're constantly tugging it back tight and running through wind tunnels, the top hairs will snap and crack off. Avoid the ponytail every day and let your hair down—go *ca-ra-zay*—every once in a while!

Best buy haircuts: Salon training

Most importantly in the quest for cheap cuts, seek out training sessions at fancy salons. All the big houses—Frederic Fekkai, Bumble and Bumble, Vidal Sassoon, and many, many more—need to train their underlings to take over the hair world when the honchos retire to beach chalets in Miami. Once a month, or once a week, the training sessions have the experts and the assistants trying out techniques—you never know whom you are going to get. At Fekkai, you could even be so lucky as to have the guru himself attend to your locks for training day prices! Why not offer up your head for a good cause: train the fellow aspiring young ladies. Plus, for more selfish reasons (let's be honest here), you just don't have the cash.

The basic info

Time: Depending on the salon, a training haircut can take anywhere from two to four hours. Remember, this is a learning process for them. It's not an in-and-out operation. Sometimes you need to spend a little time to save some cash.

Cost: At most of the training operations, you'll find you can get *fancy* cuts for killer prices, ranging from between $20 to $30. Add tip on to that and you're paying Supercuts prices for superstar quality cuts.

Common fears

"Some ambitious novice is going to trash my hair."

The real beginners aren't given weapons of destruction until they're good and ready. It's only the intermediate trainees who actually get to work on your hair. Plus, their advisors are always close by, shuttling between stations. If you sense disaster brewing, flag 'em down and feign tears. You'll get the star treatment—a teacher's cut for trainee's prices!

"I don't have daytime hours free to spend at a salon."

Many training sessions happen at night, so you don't need to take a three-hour lunch. Just call around to see what salons offer the best times, and what works best for you.

"I won't have any control over what cut I want."

Do you ever, really?

who knew?

For the best prices on quality haircuts, go multi-culti and travel. Sandra swears by getting her haircuts at a Korean salon, where the prices are significantly slashed. And Lisa only gets her hair cut in Brooklyn, where prices are far less than in the fancy salons across the East River.

chapter seven

makeup myths

t he trick to being a less-than-wealthy urban woman with taste and style comes down to one simple truth: choosing your battles wisely. Just face it. You can't have the fancy apartment, the unlimited budget for couture, the disposable income to savor wine tastings every night, the task-master personal trainer, *and* the weekly manicure/pedicure combo.

Once you settle down with that firm truth, prepare to compromise. Sift through the temptations; parse out your priorities; and choose wisely. Remember, pricier doesn't necessarily mean prettier or better quality.

The good news is that nowhere is slimming down your budget easier and more painless than in your makeup bag. That's because the true secret of the beauty industry is that, more often than not, a $20 lipstick is just a $5 one with fancy packaging. The only difference between cheap and expensive makeup is pigment quality, technology, and tube colors.

That can be a great reassurance to those of us who harbor a penchant for picking up the odd (unnecessary) lip pencil. And really, who can resist sometimes?

Sure, you're not exactly a lip pencil type. In fact, you generally tend toward a pale lipstick shade or even chapstick. But hey, that chrome *calls* to you. You think that once you buy the lip pencil, you will become a glamazon goddess—all allure, all the time. So you buy it. Fifteen dollars doesn't break the bank, but it's also more than you had planned on spending ($0).

And there you are with your new lip pencil, which you use that night before heading out to a friend's house for dinner. She doesn't notice. Like a good lip pencil should, it blends right in. And like a bad purchase, you use it twice or three times, and then go back to your quick and easy stable routine, minus the lip pencil. A smear of chapstick here, a swish of mascara, a dab of subtle color on the cheeks, and out you go.

Blame it on the chrome. Lines like Stila and Fresh, with alluring illustrations of lanky lovelies over sleek packaging, have an undeniable tug. "I'm a sucker for *anything* in chrome," admitted a former coworker named Suzanna, who'd return from many a lunch break with fresh sparkly lips and packages discreetly bundled in her bag.

It's easy to avoid the tug of well-designed tubes carrying goop you don't need. How? All you have to do is figure out what you *do* need, find out how much it's worth, and sift through the choices to get the best for the least.

WHAT DO YOU NEED?

Whether you're a simple chapstick-and-clear-mascara kind of girl or a full-on face mask type, there will be certain occasions that merit the star treatment—a job interview, a much-anticipated first date, graduation from grad school, a gallery opening.

The chapstick will get tossed for a dab of red lip gloss, your ruddy cheeks will be graced with a poof of pink, your eyelids will zing with a subtle, pale sparkly purple. And all of a sudden—voila!—you're a *gi-rl!* And no self-respecting girl should be caught without the ready supplies. So stock up ahead of time and be on your toes to make the transformation from Scrappy She-Devil to Slickster Urban Girl.

The Urban Girl's Makeup Bag
- A non-oily chapstick for everyday (I love Kiehl's Lip Balm #1)
- A pale lip gloss
- A palette of eye shadows
- A dark brown or black mascara, depending on your coloring
- A do-me lipstick (red is always a good bet)
- Perfect shade of concealer
- Foundation
- Nail polish (in clear and pale pink)
- A set of makeup brushes
- Go-with-everything lipliner
- Tweezers
- A compact with a clean, non-distorted mirror

Savor a splurge or two

Makeup counters can be like a budgetary black pit. Wandering through Macy's, disappointed with what's on the racks, you decide to head out of the store. But no. You're captivated by some display of eye makeup, sparkly creams, or scented sunscreens. You try a dab or two…and you're sold! Say bye-bye to $15. Avoid the impulsive purchases of makeup you don't need by not denying yourself the splurges that you feel you do.

My friend Karmen has one lipstick she can't do without. It's a deep red shade from Laura Mercier. The lipstick costs more than $20, but that doesn't faze her. First of all, exacting for the occasional lost bag or smushed tip, lipstick isn't something you tear through. It tends to last for at least six months. Secondly, it's Karmen's main makeup splurge; almost everything else in her makeup bag came straight from the local drugstore.

Karmen will spend the cash because it's her money-in-the-bag makeup treat. She knows it's the perfect shade for her. She knows it stays on her lips past the morning cup of coffee. And she knows that if she didn't spend $20 on that particular splurge, she would opt for at least two other $10 lipsticks that don't satisfy nearly as much. "I like the color, it lasts, and it looks good," says the thirtysomething freelance beauty editor in Michigan. "I buy it again and again." So it's a no-brainer. Every girl should have her one surefire treat. But make sure to keep it to one! You can't have seven "my one splurge" things.

THE GOO GOODS

Remember, whether you do your shopping in the drugstore or the department store, you'll be buying essentially the same goop, shimmer, and shine. From Bonne Bell to Bobbi Brown, the goo in the tubes is all just makeup: there's some oils, some coloring, some paste, and some packaging. So know where to invest in the best goo, and where to go for the cut-rate choices.

Worthwhile splurges
- Perfect shade lipstick
- A well-formulated balm
- A foundation that blends seamlessly into your skin tone
- A good set of makeup brushes

Solid scrimp cosmetics

After your one-splurge treat, you need to follow through on the bargain by paring down the rest of your price points. But it's easier than you think. There are surprisingly easy places to save cash in your makeup bag. While you splurge for the tried and true lipstick, not everything needs to be a *special* item. Where should you devote the cash and where can you go for the dime store bargains? Here are **six saving solutions**:

Facewash

Ditch the fancy Face Milk Makeup Remover ($17.99). Dermatologists swear by the humble dime store Cetaphil. It moisturizes and cleans gently. Best of all, the soap generally costs around $5 at any drugstore.

Facewashing tidbit: Keep water temperature from scalding, which will irritate skin, and pat face dry to avoid chafing post-wash.

Nail polish

All of the designer lines stock their own nail polishes for upwards of $10 a tiny bottle. Pass the pricier polishes over for dime store fare. Nail polishes

washing makeup brushes

Once you've invested in a set of beautiful brushes, it is essential to maintain their soft bristles and shape and make sure they last a long time. Brushes should be washed once a week.

Put some liquid soap in the palm of your hand. Mix with water, and swirl brushes around in it.

Rinse thoroughly in lukewarm water.

Lay some paper towels down on the side of a table, and hang the brushes over the edge, so that as they dry, they maintain their shape and the air can permeate all bristles.

have a limited lifespan as it is, since the minute you open the bottle, the varnish starts to harden, and really, how often do you do your nails anyway? By the time the $10 bottle is all caked and done, will you have gotten your money's worth? Chances are, no. Devote your resources where it'll pay off better.

Nail polishing tidbit: To make the polish last, use a basecoat of clear polish under the color and, if done correctly, the polish should last for seven to ten days. Likewise, a good pedicure should last three to four weeks.

Moisturizer

A gourmet grade moisturizer—from Lancôme, Clinique, Estée Lauder, or another one of the elite cosmetics companies—is a veritable investment. You could find yourself shelling out between $20 to $50 for a bottle that lasts a few months. Is it necessary? Not necessarily. In her book, *Don't Go to the Makeup Counter Without Me*, cosmetics industry watchdog Paula Begoun informs us that a top-of-the-line moisturizer from a fancy company like Aveda is comparable to the top-of-the-line moisturizer from Almay. Woo-hoo!

Find a satisfactory comparable moisturizer at the drugstore in Neutrogena. They all have the same ingredients anyway. You'll want one that's oil-free, to prevent zit-fests on your face; preferably look for one with a 15 SPF moisturizer to protect from sun damage. The better price? Five to ten dollars. That's more like it.

Moisturizer tidbit: Apply moisturizer first thing in the morning, just after having washed your face; your slightly damp skin will absorb more of the cream.

Mascara

Like lipsticks, these makeup bag items can dramatically range in price points. But is it necessary to devote double digits for the lash booster? One guess...no. Makeup enthusiasts

who knew?

Estée Lauder, the namesake of the powerhouse cosmetics company, received the wrath of her dermatologist uncle back in the day for using plain old soap to wash her face. *Shame, shame.* She then went on to hawk creams and makeup at posh boutiques and salons around Manhattan, launching her line. If Lauder did it, why not you?

who knew?

When in the market for a self-tanner, you're safe with the cheaper fare. As long as the product has dihydroxyacetone in it, the browning ingredient, the product should work.

secretly swoon for the humbler fare in Maybelline Great Lash Mascara. Why not follow the expert advice and save yourself a buck or ten?

Mascara tidbit: To avoid clumping, make sure the wand has only a thin layer of mascara on it and use gentle, slow, small swipes, moving outward from the lid with each swipe.

Toner

A daily face-washing routine can involve limitless number of products. There are a number of steps—wash, exfoliate, tone, treat, and moisturize—all of which could require a $30 treatment. As we're learning, though, drugstores deliver with bountiful quality. For example, instead of devoting money to fancy toner, opt for witch hazel. The natural botanical works wonderfully, for a couple of dollars a bottle.

Witch hazel tidbit: Put a bottle in the refrigerator during the summer months; when you come home sweaty and spent, dab a saturated cotton ball all over your face. Ahhh.

Petroleum jelly

Like tissues and Kleenex, copier machines and Xerox, bandages and Band-Aids, we're inevitably drawn to the name brands. But petroleum jelly is an Urban Girl's bathroom secret. She uses it instead of Vaseline on her elbows, on her hands, on her tootsies, on her heels, and even on her face if she lives in arctic regions like Manhattan wind tunnels, the Northeast, or Chicago...or San Francisco during the summer months.

Petroleum jelly tidbit: When dyeing your hair at home, apply a layer of jelly around the hairline, which will prevent the color from bleeding onto your forehead.

Department store splurges turn to drugstore scores

Like designers that have runway level couture lines and the more afford-able ready-to-wear, cosmetics companies often carry two versions of their products. Estée Lauder owns Jane; Lancôme owns L'Oréal. That means that the companies on the lower price point have access to the technology, testing, and oftentimes ingredient formulations their fancier siblings use in the expensive products.

Shop high, buy low

Find out who owns whom and then dive into the research. Head to the department store to figure out what you like. Have someone at one of the counters do your colors so you can identify what color palette is best for you. Take a sample of the perfect *you* foundation or lipstick on a Q-tip and head to the drugstore.

Mix and match

If you found an Estée Lauder concealer that was the ideal shade for your skin tone, try to match it up with the Jane concealer at the local drugstore or superstore like Target or Wal-Mart. Chances are, the two lines, owned by the same company, will have similar shades.

who knew?

Sick of your everyday lipstick color but wary of plunking down $10 to $15 for a new shade? Increase your options by doubling up, like the savvy girls in *Kissing Jessica Stein*. First lay down a thin layer of one shade, and blend in the second or third. Consider your lips a palette, and experiment one evening with all the possible color combinations.

Cash in on return policies

Since many drugstores are sticklers for keeping their goods firmly suction-sealed in packaging, inquire about their return policy before buying. That way, if the color doesn't come out quite right on your skin under natural rather than fluorescent lights, you won't have to spend double the money to get the right product. Remember, you can always play up the competition between two stores. *Well, Rite Aid will let me take it back....*

REPLENISHING AND REPLACING

Confession: There is a wand of mascara in my makeup bag that's been sitting there for upwards of three years. Three years! In my everyday makeup routine, I normally throw on a little chapstick and some pale eye shadow. The mascara only makes an appearance on weekends or special occasion weeknights when I'm going all out and want to accentuate my long blonde lashes.

I know I'm breaking with cosmetics code. I read all the magazines; I watch the Style Network; I normally dutifully heed expert advice. I'm well aware that many say I should trash my three-year-old mascara and exchange it for fresh fare. In fact, I hear that you're supposed to replace mascara every three months. But is that really true? If I did trash my mascara every three months, I'd probably only get a handful of uses out of each wand.

So is the three-month trash rule an unnecessary dumping? In many cases: yes. Unless you have a gross goo coming out of your peepers, ditch the mascara-dumping mandate for these three surefire signs of expiration:

Sharing: If you find out your grabby roommate has honed in on your mascara, chuck it. Your eye is a mucous membrane. And that's an easy way to transmit illnesses, including pinkeye and viruses.

Smell: So far, so good with my vintage mascara. It slides right on, the goop is still moist, like new. But if you notice that your makeup has developed a curious odor, that's a good sign that it's time to trash it. The formulation has aged. And unlike a good Bordeaux, it does not get better with years.

Change in consistency: If your mascara gloops, your powder significantly clumps and dries, and your lipstick cracks and hardens, it's clearly time to replace the old supplies.

INVEST IN TECHNIQUE

Now that you've found great buys at the drugstore, it's especially important to stock up on quality supplies. If you have a beauty toolbox filled with the best applicators, your dime store fare will look just as fancy as the more expensive items.

Brushes

When my friend Sari turned twenty-one, her grandmother bestowed her with a beautiful set of makeup brushes in a silk case with a delicate ribbon tie from Saks Fifth Avenue. "Every woman needs a beautiful set of makeup brushes," Sari's grandmother declared. *How true.* I ran out and invested in my own soon thereafter. At the very least, you'll need a blush brush, a thin lipstick brush, and an in-between one for the eyes. While you could certainly spend a few hundred dollars on brushes with bristles made from the chin hairs of extinct yaks, a mid-level set will do just fine. Spend no more than $60 to $80 on your set; you could probably find a nice set of brushes for a little less, perhaps around $40. With a beautiful set of brushes, your makeup will go on evenly and exquisitely.

Tweezers

Tweezers are some of the most important tools a girl can have. A five o'clock shadow on a girl's eyebrows is an easily avoidable faux pas as long as she has a competent pair of these tools. This is one area where price really corresponds with quality, so invest in the best because it will pay off. A good pair of tweezers will pull hair firmly, lie comfortably in the hand, and square off at the two tops in perfect alignment. Some people prefer square tips, others like diagonal. Personally, I prefer diagonal because I find that I

TIP: best budget beauty buys (look no further than the corner drugstore):

For skin care: Neutrogena, Pond's, Cetaphil
For haircolor and highlighting: L'Oréal
For makeup: Jane, L'Oréal
For lip balm: Blistex
For facial moisturizer: Eucerin face protective
   moisture lotion with SPF 25
For moisturizing needs: Neutrogena Body Oil

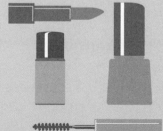

can get a great hold on hairs. Simply avoid triangle tips and you'll do fine. They don't work as well as the other two. You can find a really terrific pair of tweezers for between $15 and $20. Top-of-the-line tweezers are like excellent knives; you can send them back five years down the line to get them rehoned. So paying a little extra will certainly have its benefits.

FARMING OUT THE MAINTENANCE

Once you've figured out what you can buy at the drugstore, what your one makeup splurge is, and what high-end fare you'll fill your beauty toolbox with, it's important to figure out what services you'll do yourself and what you will head to the experts for.

The two most important regular forms of personal maintenance are waxing and having your nails done. When my brows are out of control, it's summer and I'm desperate for a dip but can't put on a bathing suit until I attend to my bikini line, my feet are callused and dry, or my fingernails are chipped at the tips and dotted with white circles, I truly feel like my life has spiraled out of control. *I can't even take care of myself. Look at me; I'm a mess,* I'll wail. But if it's the end of the month, or I'm waiting for a check, sometimes I don't have the option to put myself in reassuring, expert hands. Sometimes, a girl has to take measures into her own hands. Whether you decide to head to the salon or your bathroom, here's a budget-minded guide to important personal maintenance.

who knew?

If packaging is a big selling point, do it yourself. Buy Suave shampoo and put it in a beautiful chrome bottle. Transfer your $3.00 translucent powder into a vintage compact. Make your beautifying an aesthetic experience.

Hair removal
Home
Eyebrows: Use your tweezers to tame that thicket above your eyes. Aim to create an arch that follows the natural line of your eyes. Shape your brows so your arch lies ¾ of the length of your eye. Avoid overplucking

and coming up with bald spots by stopping every few seconds to get a look at the big picture by stepping back. For best results, keep your line neat by plucking the little hairs each morning as they arrive.

Upper lip: Waxing your upper lip could be a disaster in the making. At the end of the day, you could have a sore, red blotchy mustache instead of a dark, hairy one. Bleach instead. Buy a mild bleach at the drugstore and make sure to test on a hidden part of your body before taking the plunge on your face.

Bikini line: If you find that shaving creates a nasty nest of irritated, itchy, burning bumps, try shaving in the direction of the hair growth. Add a thick layer of soothing aloe or baby oil right after, and lie around in a robe for a little while to let the oil absorb before putting on clothes.

Legs: Shaving is a tried and true solution for leg hair. Make sure to use a thick layer of either soap or shaving cream, and moisturize generously afterward.

Salon

Eyebrows: There's no doubt about it, a good eyebrow wax can drastically improve the shape of a face. But the $10 to $20 service—*rrrripppp!*—can be a budget-breaker if you head back every time a new wee hair sprouts up. Treat your eyebrow waxes like haircuts; maintain in between and you will be able to prolong the time before your next visit. That means inspecting closely every single day to catch the new hairs as they pop up. As long as you can keep the general line of your expert eyebrow waxer, you can go as long as a few months!

Upper lip: Like any other kind of waxing, once you get started, you become tied to a cycle. As long as you can, avoid waxing your lip because an incoming stubbly 'stash is harder to hide than one with roots. This is an easy service to turn down.

Bikini line: In the summer months, a good bikini wax is a must. But if you pluck in between, like with your brows, you can keep your salon attendance down to two to three visits a season.

Legs: This is the ultimate splurge, especially considering that shaving is so easy. You're in the shower every day—just take a few swipes and you're done with it. Don't devote the cash to leg waxing.

Manicure/Pedicure

Home

A nail file, some clippers, a clear polish, and your color of choice is all it takes to treat yourself right with a manicure or pedicure at home. Start by filing your nails. Always go in one direction rather than back and forth. Take off any old polish with a cotton ball. Soak in warm (not hot) water with a few drops of vegetable oil (corn, coconut, and olive work well). Apply a base coat and then two coats of color. Allow enough time to dry. Wait five minutes before applying your top coat to ensure the coat lasts the longest. At the end, if you're in a rush, a thirty-second ice cold water plunge will speed the process. Done right, polish should last seven to ten days before you need to change it.

Salon

Having your fingers or tootsies attended to is an undeniable pleasure. It's not just about the end process (color on nails), but about getting there. The hand massage, the foot scrub, the vigorous sloughing, the overheard juicy conversation. Splurge on a salon manicure or pedicure every so often and you really will feel like you are a queen. And you are, your highness. New Yorkers have the advantage here, with really cheap nail salons on practically every block. But for Urban Girl girls in other cities, maintain in-between visits by buying the same color your manicurist uses (or bringing in your own bottle) and touching up the minute you find a smudge or a chip. Using a pumice stone in the shower will also smooth out calluses.

who knew?

A metallic polish generally lasts longer than a non-shimmery one because it contains mica, a mineral that acts like a glue on your nail, ensuring that the color sticks.

From the fridge to your face: Beauty recipes

Before celebrity stylists, before $25 face creams, and before Botox (remember those days?), girls like us would still beautify. How? We'd get crafty and do it ourselves, whipping up cosmetics recipes using what we found in the fridge, the pantry, the supply closet, and the toolbox. Stop reminiscing, tie on that apron, and get busy.

Olive oil
Mixed with sugar or salt, olive oil can be an exfoliant. In hair, it can be a moisturizing deep treatment. Apply after a shower, swath your head in a warm towel and leave for ten to fifteen minutes, and then rinse thoroughly.

Oatmeal
For a homemade mask, mix either oatmeal or cornmeal with water and apply in a thin layer on your face. Leave on to dry until skin tightens. Then rub off firmly with your hands. Follow with a thorough wash.

Dishwasher detergent
Heavily diluted, a lemony liquid detergent can work well as a cleanser for women with oily skin, though others will certainly find it too harsh. You can also use a mild lemony dishwashing detergent as a substitute for bubble bath. Dishwashing liquid can also be used as shampoo if you follow the wash with a thorough rinse with water.

Lemons
Dab a little fresh or bottled lemon juice on blemishes two to three times a day. It will dry them out and clear up skin.

Eggs
Remove the yolks and smooth the whites over your face for a mask. Lie down until it dries. Rinse with water.

who knew?
Sure, fire engine red is *caliente* for summer fingers and toes. But a subtler shade will mask chips and smudges longer.

Salad dressing
A dressing with peppercorns or poppy seeds will work well as a natural exfoliant on the face, knees, elbows, or feet. Massage into moist skin and follow with a thorough wash.

Mayonnaise
For a conditioner on dry hair, use a half-cup of mayonnaise in unwashed hair. Cover for fifteen minutes with a shower cap to allow moisturizing effect. Rinse thoroughly and shampoo.

SEASONAL COLOR CHOICES

Magazines may insist on a color rehaul with the change of seasons—*summer's here, it's time for bronze, shimmer, and yellows!*—but really, who changes their color palette with the seasons? Sometimes, on a crisp sunny, spring day, I'll dive into my pinks for a flowery boost on my cheeks and eyelids. But it usually ends at that. If you are so inclined to follow makeup trends, choose wisely, buy cheaply, and then feel free to go crazy. It is possible to transition from warm to soft colors with only the slightest change.

Season	You want	Try
Fall	driven, serious	oranges, browns, deep yellow
Winter	warm, soothing	browns, purples
Spring	hopeful, fun	pinks, peaches
Summer	light, playful	bronze, shimmer, yellow

If you plan on taking part in any makeup trends, from shimmer to bold color choices, be sure to buy at the drugstore rather than the beauty counter. You can try out new looks without spending too much money. Invest in tried and true staples rather than fly-by-night trends.

MULTITASKING MAKEUP

Your makeup bag is overflowing with smudged pencils, lipsticks, powders, concealers. Consolidate, my friend. If you head to the mirror with fistfuls of products, sprucing up will be more daunting than delightful. Lots of makeup can be used for dual purposes. Try the combos.

Use your	As
bronzer	eye shadow
pale pink lipstick	blush
brown mascara	eyebrow pencil

who knew?

In addition to using one kind of makeup for another purpose, some girls like employing art supplies. Summer, an illustrator in Brooklyn, takes cheap charcoal pencils from art stores and uses them as lip pencils.

EAT & DRINK
section three

chapter eight

drink your way into a savings stupor

"My main concern in my twenties was how I going to pay for my alcohol. With food, you could always have a cheap bagel or hot dogs, but the alcohol was the main thing money had to be spent on."
—Debbie Stoller, editor in chief of *Bust* magazine

"Keep going to the same places—and bring your friends. They'll start sending you dessert or a drink."
—Wendy Wasserstein

Sometimes, a girl just needs a drink. Period. And when that time comes, it is best to have Her Drink.

An Urban Girl's drink is like her signature scent (Fresh's Sugar); the novel she rereads every summer (*Great Gatsby*); or her steady stable of reliable stores, where she knows she can get the perfect white T-shirt (Gap, Urban Outfitters).

Her cocktail is something to rely on, to order up without having to search frantically through the mental Rolodex of drinks after finally winning the attention of bartenders (*err, I'll have a, um...can you come back to me?*).

Among my friends, Angela's drink is Tom Collins; Lisa's is Gin and Tonic; Emily's is Campari, Soda, and Grapefruit. As for mine, well, I'll admit I'm a little flitty. Over the past year, it's changed from Manhattan (Winter) to Dirty Martini (Fall) to Blood and Sand (Spring) to Caipirinha (Summer). I'm generally faithful to one for a series of months, until, like I do with my favorite album of the moment, it becomes played out, I lose my taste for it, and my attention shifts to the next Tastemaker.

Slinky Lounge Lizards

Living in a city and having a social life makes getting together tricky. My friends and I work jobs on opposite ends of town, we live well beyond walking distance, and our apartments are so small there is often only seating for two—on a loveseat in the living room. Cozy up....

So making a date with a few people at once means going out. And going out means spending money. The rote repertoire of options all involves some variation of putting something in your mouth, sipping or chewing, and swallowing. Rinse, repeat.

The obvious choices are 1) dinner, 2) drinks, or 3) coffee. For the price-conscious Urban Girl, dinner anywhere else but the corner take-out joint is a splurge. And coffee in a fluorescent-lit Starbucks well past 9 P.M. reminds this Urban Girl of too many high school weeknights with my friend Sarah, self-indulgently musing on boyfriends, UC Berkeley frat parties we'd snuck into, and how we couldn't *wait* for college, all over lattes on a street corner in San Francisco's Noe Valley. Not exactly the picture of *par-tay!*

So drinks often become the obvious choice. But spending a night cozied up to a bar usually means you'll be paying the price. Sure, there's the fistful of popped Advil and sheepish phone call reminiscences: *Did I really say that?* But the literal price is also an unpleasant kicker. A night out for drinks can be anywhere from $20 to $100.

Sure enough, a night at a bar can be a tornado to your budgetary bottom line. With beer goggles firmly planted on, you throw caution to the wind. The drinks are a-flowin', the friends are buzzing about, and there's that mysterious man making eyes across the room. The night has promise; the clock curiously stops at 10:30 P.M.

Hell, I'll have another! And one more, you toss off with a flip of the old loose wrist, *why not!?* With every intention of only having one, at the end of the night you realize you've spent three times the amount you planned on. And all you have to show for it is a dry mouth, bruised mascara line, and a deflated wallet.

Urban Girl, do not despair, and do not resign yourself to many nights at home, hugging

TIP: don't do it drinks

After *Sex and the City* aired, every Urban Girl went loco for Cosmos. *I'm like Carrie, and you're like Samantha!* But these days, the Cosmo craze is thankfully over. Similarly, there are certain drinks no self-respecting Urban Girl should order. Drinks are included on this list because the Urban Girl doesn't even care for the taste so much; she simply likes the name, or the image the name conveys, or the color, which matches her dress. Here, a partial list:

- Cosmopolitan
- Long Island Iced Tea
- Sex on the Beach
- Kamikaze

- Wine, chilled with ice cubes (red or white)
- Lite beer in a bottle

the ol' bottle. There are alternatives. First, brainstorm other options for your get-togethers.

Hour

Happy hour can indeed put a smile on the budget-minded babe's well-groomed face. In his collection of essays, *Fraud*, David Rakoff writes of his days as an assistant in the publishing world in "Lush Life," frequenting happy hours with his crew of wannabe Algonquin table members: "Dinner and forgetfulness all for ten dollars." Wendy Wasserstein recalls strategically picking out the best happy hours with friends. "We would go at cocktail time and eat all of the hors d'oeuvres." Sounds good to me!

Follow suit and scour the streets for the best happy hours. To be the best, they should have some, if not all, of these elements:

- Significant reduction in prices for all drinks, not just well drinks
- A platter of food that extends beyond carrot and celery sticks
- Some element of tiki
- A good jukebox
- No one else there besides you and your friends competing for the nourishment
- A bartender so desperate for the company he/she begins further discounting the drinks
- Air-conditioning in summer and a fireplace in winter

Gallery openings

A bar isn't the only place to convene to tie one on with friends. Next time you're planning a rendezvous, scour the local newspaper arts listings and search out gallery openings. Get some *cul-tcha* with your cocktails. Swirl wine in a glass, nod understandingly, and offer up demure, appreciative smiles to gallery owners. The openings are often early in the evening; most provide free wine and seltzer and cheese and crackers to satiate the art-loving attendees. Whether it's photography, printmaking, paintings, ceramics, sculpture, or avant-garde performance pieces, you'll come away not only having seen something new, but also with some free wine!

Word to the wise: When at a gallery opening, enjoying the bounteous bottles of wine, if you are asked for an opinion of said art, and you either 1) don't like it or 2) don't have any opinion whatsoever, then toss this off: "I find it very interesting," while staring intensely at said work. Turn back, smile, nod, and return the question.

Save more money

If going out to a bar after happy hour with several friends is the plan of action, you still have ways to cap your cocktail expenditures. Here is a list of options and general strategies.

Cocktails should never be pounded

Sip, swill, savor your drink. You'll enjoy the flavors more, and it will last longer. Try having *a* drink rather than four. There is no need to match the defcon speed of your thirsty companion.

Jane never has more than one drink when she goes out. She would much rather devote her money to Marc Jacobs than Manhattans. So Jane drinks ponderously, sipping her way through a night.

When ordering your one drink of the night, you can splurge on a wonderful cocktail with top shelf liquor. You'll really enjoy one satisfyingly strong Maker's Mark Manhattan much more than three watered-down gin and tonics anyway. When I know I'm trying to keep my night to a one-drink maximum, I'll order a cocktail without mixers, so that there's no risk of it not being strong enough: Martini, Manhattan, Mint Julep.

Pack wisely

Tracie has a fun strategy for solving the cocktail conundrum. With a very small budget and many friends to see, she came up with her own—albeit slightly shady—alternative. Before heading out to her favorite bar in Brooklyn, she stops at a corner store and picks up a six-pack of beer. In her large tote, she has stashed a sweater, to make sure the bottles don't clink, and a bottle opener, conveniently attached to her key chain. Tracie parks it on a couch, discreetly places her bag beneath her legs, and, sleuth-like, drinks away.

She got in trouble only once before, when she busted out Red Stripe, a beer the bar didn't stock. It was a dead giveaway she hadn't bought the bottle at the bar. "You're always safe with Heineken or Budweiser," she advises. Also, make sure the bar is fairly crowded so that you're not too conspicuous popping caps and slinging back longnecks.

Pre-game
There's certainly something to the whole parking lot pre-game tailgating fiestas. Take the action and turn it into your girly variety. Have a friend over for a drink before you head out, if your destination is in your neighborhood. Better yet, sip something before setting out. Sometimes, when I'm going out to an expensive lounge where the cocktails hover around $10, I'll have a tall glass of wine with dinner at home, to get my drink on for free and get my own party started.

Drink locally
If you're headed to a bar with one hundred beers on tap, avoid ordering a glass of pinot noir. It seems obvious, but follow suit with a venue's specialty. Drink locally, and drink in season. Follow the deals and it will pay off.

Say your pleases and thank yous
An Urban Girl always holds herself with the utmost poise, even when she is getting no love or attention from a crowded bar. When given the nod, she love-bombs the bartender. At the least, it will make their job more pleasant. At best, she may get a free drink out of it. Though that is not her primary motive now, is it?

WINES:
YOU SURE KNOW HOW TO PICK 'EM
Confronted with a wall of wines, most people have a sure-fire way of selecting the night's bottle. Where's the $10 rack? You may feel, as you

pony up to the register with your $8.99 Shiraz, that you are resigned to buying a B-grade bottle, within the $10 cap.

Think again. In her definitive book *Andrea Immer's Wine Buying Guide for Everyone*, Immer, master sommelier and wine columnist for *Esquire*, assures her readers that a $20 bottle is often not twice as good, or even better for that matter, than its $10 alternative. That's news we like to hear! There are excellent wines well within the Urban Girl budget. The key is figuring out which ones they are.

who knew?

If you pop a cork and aren't pleased with your purchase, take it back to the wine store with your receipt. Shop owners can return bad bottles to their distributor and you can exchange it for a better bottle. There's no need to suffer through gross glasses.

Wine primer

Gewürztraminer—your companion spits off the words deftly—and you say, "God bless you." Wrong answer. The Urban Girl must know the basics about wine to make sure she can pick the best bottles off the shelf, and have some preferences when confronted with a restaurant's wine list. (Clue: always opting for the second to cheapest bottle is not necessarily the best way to pick 'em.)

Urban Girl wines within her budget

When in doubt, search out these solid, gently priced company's bottles:

- Australia's Rosemount Estate
- BV
- Concha Y Toro
- Georges Duboeuf
- Turning Leaf
- Rabbit Ridge

Wine storage

Polishing off a bottle in one sitting, solo, certainly saves precious counter space, but it also might be a sign of a, well, *larger* problem. It's more likely (and healthy) that you'll pop a cork, pour out a glass or two, and then save the rest to last, for tomorrow. But I've accidentally aged some of my open bottles, leaving them open for over a week. And one thing is for sure: an open bottle doesn't become a prime vintage after aerating for a few weeks.

the urban girl's wine guide

Chardonnay
What: rich, fruity white
Pair with: almost anything
Drink: well chilled
Try: BV Coastal, Columbia Crest,
    Gallo of Sonoma, Macon-
    Lugny Les Charmes, R.H.
    Phillips, Rosemount Diamond,
    Turning Leaf

Sauvignon Blanc
What: acidic, tangy white
Pair with: ethnic foods and fish
Drink: chilled
Try: BV Coastal, Clos du Bois,
    Columbia Crest

Pinot Grigio
What: crisp white
Pair with: salads, salty foods,
    hors d'oeuvres
Drink: well chilled
Try: Turning Leaf, Folonari

Riesling
What: fruity white
Pair with: sushi, Indian food,
    seafood
Drink: slightly chilled, not icy
Try: Beringer Johannisberg,
    Columbia Winery
    Cellarmaster's Reserve

Merlot
What: soft, fruity red
Pair with: cheese, roasted meat
Drink: cool room temp
Try: BV, Concha Y Toro, Ecco
    Domani, Gossamer Bay,
    Mouton-Cadet

Beaujolais
What: juicy, grapey red
Pair with: anything from seafood
    to game
Drink: slightly chilled
Try: Duboeuf Beaujolais-Villages
    and Beaujolais Nouveau

Chianti
What: spicy, hardy red
Pair with: anything Italian
Drink: room temperature
Try: Santa Cristina Sangiovese,
    Cecchi

Pinot Noir
What: smoky, fruity red
Pair with: anything
Drink: cooled, but not chilled
Try: Duck Pond, Meridian,
    Turning Leaf

Cabernet Sauvignon/Blends
What: full, oaky red
Pair with: beef, lamb, anything
    heavily spiced
Drink: room temp
Try: Black Opal, Rosemount

Shiraz
What: sweet and spicy red
Pair with: cheese, grilled veggies,
    fish
Drink: room temp
Try: Black Opal, Duboeuf,
    Rosemount Diamond Label

Zinfandel
What: bold, oaky red
Pair with: meat, spicy foods,
    cheeses
Drink: room temp
Try: Rabbit Ridge, Fetzer Valley,
    Vendange

In fact, you either have to toss it or move it to your spice rack for spicing up stews or forming reduction sauces.

Perhaps it was my storage technique? I've stuffed crinkled aluminum foil in an open bottle of Chimay, hoping the carbonation stays overnight; I've crammed a cork far down in a bottle of red and placed it back on the wine rack; I've tried a fancy blown glass bottle stopper on white wine and placed it in the fridge. What works best?

For reds. Close up the bottle with the original cork or rubber stopper and place in refrigerator. Yes, the refrigerator. While the kitchen counter works as well, cooling down the wine will slow down the aeration, which ages wine for the worse. When you're ready to pour another glass, you can always leave the glass or bottle out to warm up to room temperature. *Top lifespan of open bottle: just under a week*

For whites. Stop with original cork or stopper with one-way valve and place in refrigerator. *Top lifespan of open bottle: three to four days*

For sparkling. Invest in a clamshell stopper with clamps at the local hardware or grocery store. Tightly seal to retain all carbonation, place in refrigerator. *Top lifespan of opened bottle: over a week*

COFFEE CONUNDRUM

Early on, I developed a powerful thirst for a strong cup of coffee. With a cup of coffee in the morning, everything I wrote became immediately publishable. I was an expert. My computer was my vehicle of genius. I'd jot off letters I'd been meaning to attend to for weeks. Nothing could stop me, until, an hour later, the buzz wore off, I looked back at what I'd written, and pressed BACKSPACE, hoping none of my coworkers had peered at my screen.

In high school, the theater club types and the literary journal groupies were the first to get vocal about the difference between "good and bad" coffee. *Pew!* they'd exclaim, performatively, their faces all agrimace as they sipped away at the cafeteria coffee. And then they'd go back for a refill and gripe some more about how it was really water, how hard could it be to make a good cup? I soon caught on, joining them in an appreciation for the sharp, spicy, cut-through-the-tongue-hair cup of coffee, the kick-your-ass cup. I even became a member of the well-attended club: disgruntled former Starbucks employees (*not another damn Frappuccino!*).

At my first job out of college, a dot com I worked at for about five minutes, the office had Starbucks coffee beans delivered, and my job—among other things—involved making it. My next three jobs also included the coffee perk. I came to believe coffee was like health insurance or a working phone: a workplace staple.

That is, until I started working at an alternative weekly newspaper in Boston. *Soooo*, I asked my deskmate on the first day, *where can I find the coffee?* Uh, there's a Dunkin' Donuts down the block, he muttered absentmindedly. *Yeah, but where's the pot in the office?*

He looked at me, paused for a second, shook his head as if to ward off a fly, and turned back to his computer. *O-kay, destination Dunkin' Donuts.*

For the next few weeks, I bought a cup of coffee on my way to work, trying out a few of the various unsatisfactory locations: Dunkin'

who knew?

Another option for leftover wine is to save it for cooking. A good way to preserve the wine for long periods of time is to freeze it in a Ziploc bag. The next time a recipe calls for wine, remove from freezer, leave out on counter until it warms up, and use as directed.

who knew?

If you fancy Jamaican Blue Mountain at $18 a pound, but don't relish the idea of always buying it, create your own lower-budget blend. Grind some of your hoity toity beans with another type: any basic house blend should mix fine.

Donuts ($1.55 a cup); hospital cafeteria across the street ($1.45 a cup); Starbucks counter in Barnes & Noble down the block ($1.65 a cup). Within a month, I'd spent $32 just on my morning cup of coffee, not to mention the added expense of the occasional mid-afternoon pick-me-up. Continuing the habit would have cost me about $400 a year on unsatisfying cups of murky brown liquid. Forget it!

I set out to find a better way to get my coffee fix.

I bought a one-pound bag of whole beans from Peet's, my favorite coffee shop from home ($12), dusted off my bean grinder, and purchased a tall chrome mug from Crate & Barrel ($15).

I got in the habit of making myself a cup in the morning, filling up the mug, and sipping my way to work on the bus. The beans would last me about two months. At that rate, including my initial investment, with the simple adjustment in my routine, I would save $300 a year. Not bad, especially since I was drinking better coffee anyway!

Caring for your coffee beans
Always buy whole beans and grind your own
When you grind beans, the flavor fades away faster. Alternately, when they're whole, they'll retain the sharper, spicier flavors. Grind them as you need them.

Refrigerate your beans
Either place the bag in the fridge or put the beans in a tin in the fridge. That way, they will remain fresher longer.

who knew?

On summer days, make sure to throw a chilled water bottle in your bag before you head out the door. Picking up a $2 bottle at a corner deli each day will cost you well over a hundred dollars over the course of a summer.

chapter nine

price–saving pantries

"You should always have four things you can make with your eyes closed. There should be no real angst between when you come home and when your meal flows out of your chopping block."

—Sheryl Julian, author of *The Way We Cook* and food editor of the *Boston Globe*

W e've all been there. It's 7 P.M., you've just come home from work with a gnawing hunger in your belly. You head directly to the kitchen cabinets, open them, and stand there staring blankly, without a clue. *What can I make*? Sure, another bowl of cereal is an option, but as an Urban Girl, you prefer taking the path of more persistence.

Hmm, black olives, pasta, tuna, cherry tomatoes? You make a dressing and voila! In five minutes you've made a delicious summer pasta salad. Your expenditure? Under $5. Your time? Under five minutes, far less than you would have spent foraging for takeout menus, figuring out what you want, ordering, and waiting for the delivery guy to make his way over (twenty plus minutes and about $20, with tip).

Best of all, cooking is something that you become more comfortable with the more you do it. There's a confidence to cracking open cabinets, surveying the loot inside, and being able to whip up a wonderful meal. In fact, in matters of the kitchen, impulsivity, inquisitiveness, and a sense of humor are far more important than skill. What you don't know, you *improvise*.

And what's the worst-case scenario anyway? Your soufflé falls, your pasta is soggy rather than al dente, you overdress your salad. If something doesn't turn out, so what? Laugh it off, call it a night, and order in a pizza.

As a present when I was in college, my parents gave me basic cooking lessons at the California Culinary Academy. For the entire Christmas break, I spent hours in a test kitchen, learning knife cuts, stirring risotto, and making stocks. To be honest, I was never able to recreate off the top of my head many of the concoctions we whipped up in class, but that wasn't the point. Staring down an ambitious recipe, I learned the most important thing: I can do it. And so can you.

All that basic cooking requires is the ability to read and follow instructions and the nerve to jump off the culinary cliff. If you can take the SATs, pass a driving test, or navigate a foreign city's subway system, you can become an impressively solid home cook.

While saving money may be the primary factor for you in deciding to cook rather than order in or head out for meals, once you've decided to take meals into your own hands, you'll see that this is where the fun begins.

Your first job is to make it easy on yourself. When the sun's down and the stomach growling commences, you must have the tools you need to tackle the task at hand.

Always start with a grocery list, and stick to it. A good session of grocery shopping is fundamental to lowering costs in the kitchen. Have a list of essential items that you buy every time you go. The Urban Girl can sashay through a grocery store with her eyes practically closed. At the helm of a cart, she whips around and quickly finds her basic set of essential ingredients to stock her pantry.

From there, **add on as inspiration strikes.** A fresh piece of fish; a bundle of long stalk asparagus; a half pound of bright cherries; plump tofu. But with the basics in her cart, she can whip out any number of standard recipes in her no-brainer repertoire. Her grocery cart is her culinary toolbox. She figures out her hammer, her nails, and her glue to tie everything together. That way she can come home late in the evening, push around cans in the shelf, stand in front of the refrigerator, and be able to pull something satisfying and tasty together.

SET A GROCERY SHOPPING SCHEDULE

The Urban Girl must set a grocery budget. The average American spends $36 a week on groceries, according to the Food Marketing Institute. Fifty dollars a week should be sufficient in any part of the country, though I've often been able to whittle my weekly staple budget down to as low as $35 to $40 when I have access to large grocery stores and can buy certain items generic (more on that later).

While the Urban Girl sticks to her budget, it is certainly not set in stone. Sometimes she is inspired by fresh scallops, sometimes mini artichokes speak to her. So she must retain a certain amount of financial flexibility—splurging for special ingredients occasionally—while also sticking to her grocery budget guns.

Growing up, my mother sat down every Saturday morning with recipes, a piece of paper, and a pen. She formed our complete weekly menu, day by day, and shopped accordingly to make sure we had all of the ingredients for the week's meals. While I'm not as organized in terms of anticipating what meals I'll be craving in four days' time, I like to do the same weekly shopping. It has proven to be the most cost-effective way to shop. And I've found that as long as I have my pantry staples, I can still have the space to indulge the random culinary inspirations that pop up.

Weekly shopping

The basics should be purchased on a weekly schedule and replenished in advance. The best place to do this is at a larger grocery store to get the best deals. I usually go sometime during the weekend. However, I only buy my pantry staples there.

Daily shopping

While I'll purchase my basics on the weekends at a large grocery store, I will supplement with daily shopping if I'm making a special dish, or one that requires fresh fruit, vegetables, fish, chicken, or meat. On the way home before cooking, pop into specialty markets to buy the best quality items. If you head to a fish market, you're likely to get better prices for better quality fish than you would anyway at a large grocery store.

Monthly and beyond shopping

For bulk items like paper products, seasonings, and condiments, it can be a good idea to shop a few times a year at stores like Costco, Price Club, or BJs. But since the Urban Girl doesn't have a ton of storage space, (and even if she does, she'd prefer tucking away spare chairs for impromptu dinner parties much more than thirty spare rolls of Charmin) she must know when enough is enough.

Word to the Wise: When looking for a good grocery store, be sure to find one that has a really good house brand so that you feel comfortable filling your cart with their generic products.

who knew?

Americans spend double the amount of money on food outside of the home than they did thirty years ago. While they used to devote a quarter of their entire food budget to eating out, now it's half!

SPECIAL DEALS IN SHOPPING

Greenmarket: At farmer's markets, growers come in directly to vend their products to city dwellers. It's an opportunity to get food straight from the source. In some cases, prices may still be the same as at grocery stores, but more of the profit goes to farmers. And you're getting more for your money, as the food is fresher and better. Also, an hour before closing, vendors often drop prices on wares they haven't been able to sell all day.

who knew?

Bakeries will often slash prices heavily right before closing. Head to one of them an hour before they close up shop and scoop up tomorrow's breakfast. New York's famous Zabar's Deli heavily discounts the day's bagels an hour before closing—six for a dollar. The same goes for most bakeries around the country.

Ethnic: Bodegas, Indian corner stores, and Asian markets in diverse neighborhoods are a great place to stock up on spices and indigenous foods. Next time you're in a Greek neighborhood, stock up on olives; next time you're in a Hispanic area of town, cart home all the Goya beans you can carry.

Farm stands: On a road trip through New England during the summer? Don't hesitate to pull over at the next hand-scrawled sign announcing farm-fresh foods. A box of strawberries for $1 or fistfuls of cherries in exchange for the coins in your pocket are just some of the treats you can find.

EAT SEASONALLY AND SAVE

One of the best ways to be cost-conscious through cooking is to be sure to eat seasonally and locally, advises Sarah Lydon, a food writer who has contributed to *Saveur* and *Boston Magazine*. Go for crisp cucumbers in the summer and spinach in the winter; tomatoes in the summer and kale in the winter; apples in the fall and corn in the summer. Grocery stores will put fresh fruits and vegetables on special so the prices are discounted, and the taste is dramatically better with fresh foods anyway. While you may crave a tomato in winter, both the price and the quality will be deterrents. You won't find the same plump, red, juicy affair, and the price will be significantly higher. Don't fight it. Go with the seasons, eat locally and seasonally, and you will save money in the process.

In Amanda Hesser's delightful and thorough book *The Cook and the Gardener*, she divides her stories, recipes, and instructions by the seasons, a seemingly obvious but remarkably unique way to arrange information. This book is a wonderful resource for all cooks, from the 7 P.M., hungry, get-the-job-done cook to the aspiring chef not afraid to purée, marinate, and sift with the best of them.

URBAN GIRL KITCHEN STAPLES
pantry must-haves

- Bread
- Bagels
- Coffee beans
- Dried pasta
- Rice (basmati and white or brown)
- Black beans
- Cans of tuna
- Nuts

- Olive oil
- One other kind of oil
- Balsamic vinegar
- Soy sauce
- Sugar
- Honey
- Chicken broth

- Canned whole tomatoes
- Red and white onions
- Garlic
- New potatoes
- Cereal
- Crackers

refrigerator must-haves

- Fruit, whatever is seasonal
- Vegetables, whatever is seasonal
- Cheese (parmesan and cheddar and any others)

- Juice
- Olives
- Lemons
- Tortillas
- Milk

- Eggs
- Butter
- Dijon mustard
- Mayonnaise

FROM STAPLES TO MEALS

With your pantry well-stocked, you've now positioned yourself to eat well. Better yet, your meals will be both low-cost and high-yield.

These are the puzzle pieces, but how do they all fit together? Here are a few sample recipes that I use with my pantry staples. Since I received most of my training in California and then studying abroad in Tuscany, my style, you might notice, is quite basic and simple, focusing on fresh ingredients and spices. Some of these recipes originated from books, but I've personalized them over time.

Cooking for one can be tricky. Most recipes produce enough for three or four. The ideal scenario is to make something that will continue to be delicious tomorrow and the next day. Roasting a chicken? Make two. It takes no more work and you will have double the meals. Making soup for yourself? Double up and freeze quart-sized containers for an upcoming busy week.

Most important, stop thinking of your leftovers as "the dregs." Refashion them from chilled and soggy to something entirely different, all warm and spiced up with new ingredients. For example, your roast chicken becomes chicken salad, which can also be turned into a chicken stock, which you can freeze and use for pasta or soups.

Before diving into your culinary bonanza, tie on a fun apron for inspiration, crank up some ambient music, start off with a sparklingly clean workspace, and turn your cooking into the enjoyable experience it can be. All of these recipes call for ingredients from your pantry basic staples. You have everything you need. Exact measurements aren't needed; just experiment with what you have! Now go get busy.

Pasta Puttanesca

Onion and garlic   Chili flakes
Olive oil   Can of whole tomatoes
Tuna   Olives or capers
Pasta

Sauté onions and minced garlic in chili flakes and olive oil in
    large saucepan.
Add canned tomatoes and tuna and either olives or capers.
Let simmer. Add over any kind of pasta.
Sprinkle with salt and pepper to taste.

Salad Nicoise

Lettuce   Eggs   Black olives
Capers   Tuna   New potatoes

In one large bowl, combine washed and dried lettuce, hard boiled
    eggs, olives, capers, tuna, and boiled potatoes. Mangia!

Dressing: Olive oil, Balsamic vinegar, Dijon mustard
    All vinaigrettes use the same proportions: usually three or
        four parts oil to one part vinegar. Mix accordingly.
    Add a teaspoon of mustard, plus a pinch of salt and
        pepper.

Beans & Rice doctored up

Half an onion	2 cloves of garlic	Olive oil
1 can black beans	1 can of black-eyed peas	
1 cup of chicken stock	Yellow rice	
Cheese (when possible, I like to use smoked gouda)		

Sauté onions and garlic in olive oil in a large skillet.
When they have browned, add in black beans and black-eyed peas
    and enough chicken stock to cover the tops of the beans.
Turn down the heat and let stock reduce for 15-20 minutes.
Sprinkle grated cheese on top, spice with salt and pepper, and
    serve with yellow rice.

Summer Pasta

Pasta	Asparagus	Parmesan cheese
Butter	Lemon juice	Capers

Cook pasta in boiling water until al dente.
Cut asparagus into small pieces at a diagonal line and discard
    the woody ends. Fill a shallow pan with two inches of water
    and simmer. Cook the asparagus in the water until it
    turns a bright green and is easily speared by a fork.
    Remove well before it gets soggy and the green darkens.
Place asparagus over pasta, and mix with cheese, butter, lemon
    juice, and capers to taste.

Things you should never buy, but make

It would be easy, yet costly, to always head to the store for ingredients when you need them. Instead, try making some of your own at home. Here are two things you can easily make at home with your pantry staples.

Flavored oils

If a salad calls for hazelnut oil, add olive oil and toasted hazelnuts. Instead of setting out to buy a $15 bottle of fancy oil, make your own by soaking the nuts or spices in oil for twenty-four hours.

Salad dressing

Avoid spending a few dollars on bottles of salad dressing when you can easily make your own. "If you can stir a spoon in a bowl you can make salad dressing," instructs Sheryl Julian, who is also assistant editor of *The Grand Diplome Cooking Course* with Anne Willan. Add together combinations of mayonnaise, eggs, mustard, olive oil, and vinegar in various combinations to make your own dressing. Treat the kitchen like your laboratory, and experiment on different combinations. Go crazy.

GENERIC—AN INSULT OR A GOOD IDEA?

Generic products have a bad rep. But oftentimes, they're equally as good and much cheaper than their name-brand alternatives. In fact, many times they're actually made by the same people who make the brands, on contract. Some things are worth buying generic; the key is simply knowing when the house brand works just as well.

Word to the wise: The best time to buy generic is when baking. If the food is heading straight for the oven, a blender, or a mixing bowl, spend less on the second-best because the taste is bound to change anyway and you will be mixing it with other ingredients. For example, use house-brand flour, sugar, and eggs if you use you're baking a cake, or use house-brand pasta in a tortellini soup.

Generic or low-cost winners

Barilla pasta

It's possible to find great low-cost pastas to stock your pantry. Barilla is a really solid choice that many experts, such as Amanda Hesser, swear by.

Cereal

Cereal is one thing that can be a real budget-breaker, as some favorite boxes can cost as much as $5 a carton. *Puh-leese*. Most grocery stores will offer their own generic alternatives to the big-name kinds, everything from Honey Nut Cheerios to Grape Nuts. Sample some of them to test if they satisfy in the same way as the name brands.

Bread

If you are buying a baguette to make croutons, or a Tuscan bread soup or pudding, opt for a generic baguette. But if you're looking to have a stand-alone baguette to accompany a Tuscan feast, go for the best.

What to splurge on

- A really good olive oil
- Sandwich breads
- Sea salt or kosher salt
- Herbs
- Fish and meat products
- Fresh fruits and vegetables

who knew?

Become acquainted with nuts. Toast sliced almonds in a saucepan with some olive oil to snack on; sprinkle walnuts on salads. They add elegance to a dish for very little money. Keep a can of your favorite kind in the pantry.

URBAN GIRL COOKBOOKS

With her well-stocked pantry, all the Urban Girl needs is a little bit of direction. Look to these basic cookbooks for simple, delicious, easy recipes:

- *Home Cooking*, by Laurie Colwin
- *The Yellow Farmhouse Cookbook*, by Christopher Kimball
- *A New Way to Cook*, by Sally Schneider
- *The Joy of Cooking*, by Irma Rombauer

- *Essentials of Classic Italian Cooking*, by Marcella Hazan
- *Off the Shelf: Cooking From the Pantry*, by Donna Hay
- *The James Beard Cookbook*, by James Beard

STORAGE TO KEEP EVERYTHING FRESH THE LONGEST

Once you've stocked up at the grocery store, the goal is to eat all your goodies before they grow mold or stiffen up. While some foods have an obvious shelf life, others are more mysterious. How long does flour last? How about balsamic vinegar?

Food isn't meant to live in the baggies you bring home from the supermarket. It needs an environment it can breathe in, advises *The Way We Cook*'s Julian. "After coming home from the market, I spend an hour preparing my foods for the refrigerator." Most importantly, lettuce should be washed and dried, wrapped up in paper towels, and stored in Ziploc bags. Stored as such, it will stay fresh for ten days.

Similarly, store all your foods correctly and you can maximize the lifespan to get the most use out of those bottles and jars.

TIP: keep 'em apart

Certain foods should be separated as they're stored because they produce a gas called ethylene that makes other foods bitter, soft, mealy, or tough.

Separate	From
Apricots	Apples
Bananas	Lettuce
Cantaloupe	Carrots
Mangoes	Potatoes
Kiwi	Broccoli
Tomatoes	Squash
Plums	Green beans

Storage temperatures

Yes, we know that ripening fruit should be stored in a cold refrigerator and spices in a cool, dry pantry, but what do those temperatures really mean?

Refrigerator: 40 degrees Fahrenheit or below. The dial may need to be adjusted seasonally to maintain the 40° stability. In the summer, you may

FOOD	LIFESPAN	WHERE
fruits		
Apples	up to three weeks	in refrigerator unwashed
Bananas	a few days ripe	exposed until ripe and then refrigerated
Berries	a few days	opened in refrigerator
Cherries	a few days	unwashed in crisper
Citrus fruits	a week	refrigerated
Peaches	a couple weeks	in pantry
Ripe pears	a week	in pantry
Pineapple	a week	in the refrigerator
vegetables		
Celery	up to two weeks	in crisper
Corn	a few days	in husks in refrigerator
Head of lettuce	a week	unwashed in refrigerator
Tomatoes	a week	in the refrigerator
staples and seasonings		
Butter	up to two weeks	covered dish in refrigerator
Catsup	a year	refrigerated after opening
Spices	six months	in pantry
Cornstarch	a year and a half	in pantry well sealed
Eggs	over a month	in shell in refrigerator
Milk	about a week	in refrigerator
Cheese (opened)	about a month	tightly wrapped in refrigerator
Cheese (unopened)	a few months	tightly wrapped in refrigerator
Herbs	six months	in dark, dry pantry in airtight container
Margarine	up to six months	in container in refrigerator
Pasta	up to two years	in pantry
Opened cereal	a few months	rewrap liner tightly and firmly seal box
Flour	more than six months	in airtight container in pantry

need to refrigerate more heavily to keep the temperature down, and the opposite goes for the winter.

Pantry: below 85° Fahrenheit. Your pantry should be far enough away from heavy appliances like the stove or refrigerator, which can heat up the area. Temperatures above 100° can harm canned goods.

Freezer: 0 degrees Fahrenheit. Anything above 0° isn't guaranteed to prevent spoiling organisms. Plus, the flavors, textures, and nutritional value of your food are at risk of changing.

Can it last?
Follow the temperature gauge and canned foods should last well beyond your current lease.

How long?	Canned products
Over a year	Tomatoes, dressings, fruits
Two to five years	Soups, meats, beans, peas

Word to the wise: Just because the date on a carton has passed, you don't necessarily need to toss the item in the trash. That date relates to the store's ability to sell the product, rather than your deadline to consume it. The food stays edible well beyond that date. Just recognize it as the *sell* date rather than the *spoil* date.

who knew?
Dairy goods in plastic containers, like cream cheese and cottage cheese, do best when turned upside down. On its head, the container keeps out more air, maintaining freshness longer.

TIP: to freeze or not to freeze
There are things in my freezer that are completely unrecognizable. Ground beef from last year, a slab of cake. I always start off with the best of intentions—*I will eat this at a later point*, I reassure myself—and put it in the freezer. What a wonderful technology. But intentions don't necessarily transfer to actions, especially when something as scary-sounding as *defrosting* is involved. Best rule of thumb? Be honest with yourself. Really honest. If you don't imagine eating in later, don't bother busting out the Tupperware and storing foods you're unlikely to touch.

the only 5 spices you really need

the Urban Girl considers her kitchen her own personal laboratory. There are whirring machines, smoky pots, measuring cups, metal utensils. She walks in, puts on her protective apron, surveys the instructions, and gets started trying to recreate a previous printed success.

Every meal starts with a hypothesis: you have a vision, a plan for how things will turn out. You begin, throwing in a half a cup of this, a teaspoon of that, a dash of some odd powder. And poof! Thirty minutes later, your creation emerges. Truth be told, it's often quite different from your vision. But is it better? The answer is often yes! Whimsical experimentation can lead to brilliant new inventions. And where better to patent your own creation than in the kitchen?

Any home cook adds in a dash of curiosity, a whiff of ingenuity, and a healthy pound of on-her-toes versatility. And then she crosses her fingers and hopes for the best! By the time she sits down at the table, the Urban Girl has added some of her own spice to a dish; it is duck *a la moi*, an Urban Girl stew.

URBAN GIRL COOKS ON HER TOES

There is no better approach in matters of the kitchen than flexibility and improvisation. Though you may follow a recipe's directions with an eagle eye, still, your homemade mayonnaise separates; grape leaves burn in a pan; a soufflé sags. Cooking is not an exact science. You must be ready to change courses and try new things on the fly.

The ideal is when ad libbing becomes second nature. A writer I know recently recounted a scenario to me: someone at her work approached her on a Monday morning after having used one of her recipes for Sunday dinner. The recipe was for pasta tossed with spiced raw tomatoes and bread crumbs. Simple enough.

The woman, however, realized that she didn't have angel hair pasta, so she decided to substitute penne. When she went into the refrigerator to take out tomatoes, she realized that she was completely out, so she chopped up red pepper. Then, though she could have sworn she had bread crumbs, she couldn't find them anywhere, so she threw in some croutons. By the end, it was an entirely new dish, and a delicious one at that.

And that's precisely what a good recipe should do for the home cook: give ideas and guidance. "You do what you can do given what you have on hand," says Julian. "If you don't have one of the ingredients, make your eye go to the next line."

Sarah, a food writer in Boston, tries to maintain a low budget while also cooking delicious food. "It's tough," she says, "when at the very bottom of a long recipe, it calls for a tablespoon of walnut oil." You can go out and purchase a $15 bottle of walnut oil for that tablespoon for that one recipe, or you can get crafty and find something else in your kitchen cabinet that can substitute.

That said, the Urban Girl should certainly splurge on some of her favorite ingredients. If you recognize a taste for walnut oil, if a splash of raspberry vinegar makes you feel like you're eating a civilized meal, then by all means buy it. Choose the best wisely. Pick out something that is both deeply satisfying and incorporated into enough of your dishes to make it worthwhile to you. Make it something that feels like a treat.

I put most of my special grocery budget into olive oil, purchasing the best from a store that imports oils from Tuscany and Greece. The flavor fills up a dish and I can recognize the differences in many of my creations, such as my salad dressings and my pastas. Using a rich oil, I can add the most simple toppings to pasta and it will help to bring out the flavors already there in the fresh ingredients.

SPICE RACK: A RACKET?

When was the last time you used cumin? How about coriander? Yet, you have that swively chrome or wooden kitchen counter spice rack, all filled up and ready to be pillaged. It's no surprise that most kitchen counter spice racks go untouched. They're packed with ingredients most home cooks rarely use.

Sure, a kitchen needs to be furnished, like all other rooms of the house, but a filled spice rack is one of the least cost-efficient ways to do it. There is, of course, the call of the chrome and the allure of a well-oiled polished wood unit that swivels like a Lazy Susan. But a kitchen counter should be a workspace rather than a place to decorate. It should be, first and foremost, useful and well-designed to maximize room to chop, space for cookbooks, and elbow room for plating dishes.

Instead of suavely swiveling a rack of fifty spices, which cost you upwards of $50, buy your ingredients one by one and nail in a rack on the wall, which you can decorate with a hanging vine of chili peppers.

Buy spices where you can find them in bulk, at whole foods stores and co-ops, where you can fill up plastic bags. Or head to ethnic grocery stores, where chili powder is a staple rather than a delicacy.

With a ready set of fundamental spices, rather than the abundant and excessive fifty, even the ambitious home cook will be able to tackle most types of cuisine...as long as she's willing to get her hands dirty and experiment.

The basic spices

Salt: Keep a container of sea salt on the kitchen table as the taste is much sharper and deeper those that found in most ready-filled shakers. Use simple iodized salt when boiling a pot of water or when baking: this is when a flavor should blend in rather than distinguish itself.

Pepper: Invest in a pepper grinder so that you can grind the whole peppercorns when you are read to eat. The freshly ground pepper will taste much better than the equivalent, which was factory ground long, long ago.

Curry powder: A fresh bag of curry powder from an ethnic grocery, which you keep tightly sealed, will be an invaluable resource in many dishes.

Basil: You can either buy basil dried or keep fresh basil washed and wrapped in towels in the refrigerator. Better yet, keep a basil plant in a window box so you can pluck the fresh leaves as you need them. Also, you could try an Italian seasoning mix.

Chili flakes: You could also buy chili powder, but I find that the flavor from the flakes rather than the powder is much more versatile in different dishes.

who knew?

Unless you're dealing with a curry, you can always substitute or go without the spices that the recipe specified.

Spice substitutions

When in the middle of trying out a new recipe, you may find that you are, *gasp* , without saffron. Instead of heading out to a specialty gourmet store to buy a pinch of one of the most expensive ingredients around, the Urban Girl devises another solution, one that costs significantly less, and doesn't require her to abandon ship. It's easy: she uses turmeric instead.

Sure, the taste is different. She knows that with substitutions, the taste difference is inevitable. But all in all, she knows it's good enough. The dish still satisfies, and perhaps even more so because she knows that she ad libbed her way through yet another culinary obstacle course. She has won another notch in her cutting board.

I've gathered together some tried and true substitutions from culinary experts, home cooks, and university extension experts. Read on and save yourself the hassle and unnecessary expense of a cool, swively spice rack.

standard substitutions for herbs and spices

Spice	Alternative
Basil	Oregano or thyme
Cardamom	Ginger
Cinnamon	Nutmeg
Cloves	Cinnamon or nutmeg
Chives	Chopped tops of green onion
Parsley	Cilantro
Rosemary	Thyme
Saffron	Turmeric

Kitchen staple	Alternative
1 tsp baking powder	¼ tsp baking soda + ½ cup buttermilk
1 cup chicken broth	1 bouillon cube or 1 tsp powder in 1 cup boiling water
1 tsp lemon juice	½ tsp vinegar
1 cup shortening	1 ⅛ cup butter
1 tsp Worcestershire sauce	1 tsp steak sauce

WHEN BAD MEALS HAPPEN TO GOOD PEOPLE

Every experiment is not a success.

In her collection *Home Cooking*, Laurie Colwin writes lovingly about the beauty of a failed meal. She writes, in "Repulsive Dinners: A Memoir": "There is something triumphant about a really disgusting meal. It lingers in the memory with a lurid glow, just as something exalted is remembered with a kind of mellow brilliance."

Because the Urban Girl has big ideas, from the kitchen to the office to the closet, she is ambitious: she tries new things; she substitutes spices; she makes a feast out of what she finds in her fridge; she refashions leftovers into an entirely new meal. She gets an A for effort, but sometimes an *eww* for final product.

Scene I: My Repulsive Romantic Meal

It was the first night that I was cooking for the new boyfriend. He had been treating me to his excellent dinners for weeks now, and I had been getting increasingly nervous about how I would reciprocate. I decided to go classic, with a twist. Since I was so comfortable with Italian cuisine, I opted to bake a polenta and lay chicken breasts sautéed in spiced tomatoes over the bed of polenta. Easy enough, but it also promised a certain level of *effect. Wow,* he would murmur. *You are amazing.*

Sadly, that was not the end of my culinary story. I made a fatal flaw at the very beginning of the evening. Preparing a pot to boil water in which to make the polenta, I got a little heavy-handed with the amount of salt I poured in. Ahh, I thought, no worry, things will shake out later and be offset by the other flavors in the dish.

Well, that wasn't entirely the case. The polenta was inedible. The new boyfriend was gracious about it, however. *Delicious!* He enthused. *More, please.* But I knew he was just being nice. I dumped it and put together a big salad to accompany the chicken. We laughed it off and he made dinner for me the next week.

Solution: Learn to go easy on the salt when boiling water.

Scene II: Sarah's Singed Grape Leaves

Sarah was having several people over for a dinner party. She had prepared almost everything but still had to finish off the grape leaves. Earlier in the day, she'd made the filling and rolled them up into puffs in the green leaves. She still had to cook them in a pot, a process that takes many hours. Right as she put them in the pot, her new beau called. They had a one-hour window when they could see each other. It was right at the start of the relationship when they were greedily stealing as much time together as possible (an hour here, a coffee there).

Sarah looked at her watch, looked at the grape leaves on the stove, and opted to go for it. She turned down the heat as low as it would go and took off. A couple hours later, when she raced back home from across town, she peered in the pot anxiously. The grape leaves were charred at the bottom and she took them directly from the pot into the trash.

Solution: Watch what's on your stove.

Scene III: Lisa's Sweet and Sour Experience

Lisa and Erik had just moved in together after dating for about three months. It was the second night of their first week together, and Lisa decided to make dinner for her boyfriend. Since things were still so new, and this was a special occasion, she opted for something classic, solid, well-worn: her family's favorite sweet and sour chicken, a Chinese dish. The sweet and sour chicken was a staple of Lisa's family's culinary reper-toire; every week or so, her family would enjoy the dish. It was something she felt perfectly comfortable cooking and a dish that she was eager to introduce to her boyfriend.

Erik stayed out of the kitchen while she cooked, and when they sat down to eat, she presented the dish with a Ta-Da! Erik plunged his fork in, took one bite and pronounced it inedible. He couldn't stomach more than one bite. "Is there or is there not catsup in this dish?" he wondered aloud. Lisa was horrified and terribly embarrassed; they ordered in Chinese food (no sweet and sour chicken) and she has yet to make the dish again. (They are now engaged.)

Solution: Have take-out menus at hand when cooking a new dish for someone you care about.

A SAMPLE MEAL FOR THE AMBITIOUS URBAN GIRL

Below is an example of an ambitious recipe and suggested substitutions. Tie on that apron and take the plunge. Be comfortable trying new things.

Almond-Crusted Salmon with Leek and Lemon Cream

4 tablespoons (½ stick) butter [or margarine]
3 tablespoons fresh lemon juice
1 cup whipping cream
¼ cup chopped fresh parsley [or dried cilantro, depending on what's in the fridge]
1 tablespoon grated lemon peel
½ teaspoon salt
⅛ teaspoon ground black pepper
½ cup all purpose flour
6 6-ounce skinless salmon fillets
1 large egg, beaten to blend
2 tablespoons olive oil

who knew?

Instant rice tends to be much more expensive than regular white rice, as much as four to six times, in fact. Slow down and save.

Melt butter in large pan and add leeks, sautéing until soft. Cover and cook until leeks are tender, stirring occasionally.

Increase heat and add lemon juice. Stir until liquid evaporates. Stir in cream. Simmer until slightly reduced.

Transfer to blender and blend until smooth. Strain sauce into same saucepan. Season sauce to taste with salt and pepper. Cover and refrigerate.

Mix almonds, parsley, lemon peel, ½ teaspoon salt, and ⅛ teaspoon pepper on plate.

Place flour on another plate. Sprinkle salmon with salt and pepper. Dredge salmon in flour, shaking off excess. Brush one side of salmon with beaten egg. Press brushed side of salmon into almond mixture.

Arrange salmon, nut side up, on baking sheet.

Melt 1 tablespoon butter with 1 tablespoon oil in each of two heavy large skillets over medium heat. Add half of salmon to each skillet, almond-coated side down, and cook until crust is brown. Turn salmon and sauté until cooked through and opaque in center.

Transfer fish to plates. Spoon sauce on salmon and serve.

Makes 6 servings.

Adapted from *Bon Appétit*, April 2002 issue.

I like this recipe because it calls only for eight things, all of which are pantry staples, other than the pieces of salmon, which you can pick up on the Day Of.

who knew?

Boned chicken and lamb can be at least half as expensive as its skinless, boneless alternative. Take the bone off yourself, or leave it on if you're having a quiet meal at home. Why pay double to have someone else do it? Plus, the bone tacks on flavor. When you remove it, set it aside for future use in soups and stocks.

TIP: urban girl cooking maxims

A strong cheese masks flavor. Invest in the best and add shavings to everything from your salads to your pastas.

Fresh ingredients are bound to make for a better tasting meal.

Get creative with presentation. Cut your breads in unique shapes. Arrange hors d'oeuvres in symmetrical patterns on a platter. Prepare dishes with lots of color (a spinach salad with blood orange and walnuts). Every dish presents an opportunity to beautify.

chapter eleven

entertaining for less

if you're strapped for cash, joining friends for dinner can be an astoundingly expensive affair. Even at the most moderately priced restaurant, it's hard to walk out without having spent less than $30, the equivalent of the Urban Girl's weekly grocery budget. Occasionally, however, a night out sampling a new restaurant, celebrating an occasion, or *just because*, is something the Urban Girl savors.

So you do it wisely. You forgo the before-dinner drink; you order a scrumptious large appetizer ($11), perhaps a steaming pot of mussels or calamari, and a mid-range glass of wine ($8); you decide against dessert. And you figure that the night will set you back no more than $25, with tax and a generous tip. That should be just fine; you've allocated for it in your budget. Knowing you had dinner plans for Saturday night, you were so good and made yourself lunch all week, saving the $25 you would have spent on sandwiches at the corner deli. Perfect.

And then the bill comes. One gung-ho person snatches it up—conveniently the same one who ordered four rounds, and three courses—and after a minute of mental calculations announces what the sum is for each person. "$300 divided by 6 is...$50 each. Oh, man! All I have is a $20; I'll put it on my card and you can all pay me cash."

You simply can't pipe up, and try to argue, "Well, actually, my $11 appetizer and glass of wine cost far less than that. How about I contribute $25?" That would be mortifying, déclassé, Larry David-like even. So you suck it up and pay double, huffing as you arrive home.

Is this an inevitable fate?

Sometimes, yes. The decadent dinner and the ominous bill-divide is unavoidable, but only in a few scenarios. So be prepared:

- Your best friend from high school, who is now a corporate lawyer, is having a birthday party at a chi-chi new boîte. Your absence would be an affront and potentially damaging to your relationship.
- A friend from semester abroad/from home/from summer camp is in from out of town for only two days. She is trying to gather the old crew, all ten of you, and has called to say that dinner is the set plan. *I can't wait to see you!* she enthuses on your voicemail.

- A friend of a friend, who may be able to hook you up with some plush work gig (!) or a boyfriend has offered to meet you for lunch...at Barneys. You are very grateful that she's devoted time to chat with you. Suck it up.

Otherwise, there are ways to avoid getting in to situations such as the ones above.

Decide if it is essential
If a few peripheral friends are gathering impulsively for a BBQ feast (*don't forget the bib!*), if a coworker you don't even really like asks if you'd like to grab dinner after work one night, if your grandmother set you up on yet another destined-to-be-disastrous blind date with a "nice doctor," chances are you can squirrel your way out of the engagement. If it's not a treat, then treat it like an unnecessary extra.

Be honest about your financial constraints
Just because one person has enough money to spend $50 on dinner doesn't mean everyone else in the party of six does as well. Chances are, if you are feeling stressed out and strapped, someone else at the table is, too. While you and your friends are still in the planning stages, choosing the dinner destination, don't hesitate to drop some gentle hints. "Someplace mid-range would be great!" or "I'm on a fairly low budget these days." They'll get the hint.

Emily and Scott recently bought a house and have been using that as a way to opt out of expensive restaurant excursions. "We've been on the rice and beans diet because we just bought a house," they recently said to a friend who was trying to set up a meal. "How about you come over?"

Meet for lunch, drinks, coffee, or a walk, instead of dinner.
There are a multitude of options beyond dinner for you to enjoy a social soiree. If it's a meal you'd prefer, have lunch instead of dinner; the mid-day meal is much more reasonably priced than sumptuous suppers. Offer to meet for drinks rather than dinner. You'll save at least half the money. Or

go for coffee. When in doubt, explore a new neighborhood in a walking tour; make an excursion out of it rather than popping a squat at a prohibitively expensive swank dinner joint.

Go ethnic

It just so happens that some of the most delicious foods are cheap. Brainstorming places for dinner? Suggest Thai, Mexican, Korean, or Chinese rather than French, Italian, or *anything* "fusion," which is bound to be trendy and therefore priced higher. Susan Orlean recalls when she and her first husband were living in Boston, making do on a very small budget. "We ate out, but we *only* ate at ethnic restaurants," she reminisces.

Eat at the bar

Desperate to try the new chic restaurant? Grab a friend or go solo and stake out a seat at the bar. Bars are made for breaking the rules. Order two appetizers, share an entrée—you won't have to shrug off attitude from disappointed waiters hoping to make a big tip off of your table.

Avoid big groups

In smaller groups, you can be more intimate, and therefore it's often easier to broach the topic of paying for what you ordered, rather than splitting the bill 50/50, unwittingly covering your tablemate's boozy feast.

EATING OUT MAXIMS

You've decided to go out for dinner. Now what? Opening up the menu, you can make some wise choices to cut your costs. Here are some ways and means to have your meals be meaty rather than meager.

Start out partially sated

Dina is a culinary student in New York who loves to try the new restaurants and sample trendy new dishes and spice combinations. But on her small

who knew?

At some places, such as California's wine country, patrons are permitted to take the remainders of a partly full bottle home with them. Don't be embarrassed to ask what's kosher in your neck of the woods.

stipend, it's not exactly an option. When she absolutely wants to go out, she'll have a snack ahead of time so that when she arrives at the restaurant, she's not starving and is primed to *taste* rather than devour. Dina can order a less expensive small plate rather than a round of beef to fill up her belly.

Wine and dessert

Alcohol and dessert are where restaurants make the most profit. Knowing that, opt to have these nonessentials at home with your dinner companions. Have a bottle of wine chilled and a nice pie or tart ready for the last course, *a casa*. Taking a walk and having a change of scenery can be nice, anyway, after sitting at a table for too long.

Meat v. veggie

Even if you fancy the occasional night of meat-eating, satisfy the craving at home. When ordering in a restaurant, eating a vegetarian dish is significantly cheaper than the meat and seafood alternatives.

Appetizers and sharing

If you're so inclined, join forces with your dining companions and order a few dishes for the table. Some people are quite strongly disinclined to share meals, but I find it to be a great option when eating out on limited means. Plus, you get to try more things!

Word to the wise: Never order wine by the glass at a restaurant. If you are two at the table, order a half carafe. (There are generally six glasses of wine in one bottle.) The markup on wine in a restaurant is criminal, and the markup is even higher when it comes to glasses rather than bottles. Even if you don't plan on drinking the whole bottle, you'll get your money's worth by the end of the night. Then, when there is a glass-worth of wine left in the bottle, the Urban Girl sends it back to the chef with her card, thanking him or her graciously for the wonderful meal.

EATING YOUR WORDS: DOWNSIZING YOUR DIET

You've been downsized; you've taken a smaller salary for a better job; you've started graduate school. While you may have been living the Lush Life, stopping off for takeout every evening, trying out the new restaurant of the week as they open, now it's time to cut back.

The obvious first step is a no-brainer: stop eating out so often. But how much of a difference does it actually make?

Pack your lunch/Dine in instead of out

Instead of running out for a quick salad, soup, or sandwich mid-day, pack your own. Buy a freshly baked artisanal wheat bread, a pound of lunch meat, some fruit, and a large bag of pretzels each week for $15.

Also, if your idea of a culinary excursion is racing out to the corner sushi joint and toting back some cucumber rolls to your apartment for dinner—a frugal affair, you might think—every $10 to $15 meal adds up.

Here's how much packing lunch and foregoing takeout can pay off in the long term (*just think of all the shoes!*):

	pack your own	$7 lunch	$10 lunch
A week:	$15	$35	$50
A month:	$60	$140	$200
A year:	$720	$1,680	$2,400
Save annually:		$960	$1,680

cutting out	one $15 takeout	one $40 dinner
A week:	$15	$40
A month:	$60	$160
A year:	$720	$1,920

Christina and her husband had to cut costs when she entered graduate school. So they set a weekly budget of $80 for all meals for both of them, slashing their expenses on eating out and buying groceries to last them through three meals a day. Before, they'd been spending about $300 a week on food (groceries as well as dining out) for both of them.

In one month, they saved $1,000! "I actually don't feel deprived," Christina marvels. "It was just a lifestyle change. And it's healthier; I've lost weight because I'm eating less...and better."

DINNER PARTY PRICES

Trying to avoid the ominous expensive unfair Bill Split, you decide to invite some friends over to your place for an impromptu dinner party. But in attempting to avoid overpaying for your meal, somehow you've now found yourself paying for four people's meals.

NEWSFLASH: Dinner parties are pricey! There's wine to be bought, special foods to be picked up, flowers to be arranged, the right party music to be purchased...you get the point.

I recently threw a dinner party with my boyfriend for another couple who had had us over to their apartment last year. They operate at quite a different price point than we do. She, a former editor of mine, is now a business school student and he is an art dealer. Their dinner included canapés and champagne to start, followed by a three-course meal accompanied by four bottles of wine, and a scrumptious cheese course, a palette of six artisanal local specialties. We rolled out of their apartment stunned by the succession of flavors, daunted by the prospect of reciprocating their graciousness.

When we had them over, we knew that we wouldn't be able to match the decadence of their affair, but we still wanted to put on an elegant and delicious dinner. So...$85 worth of groceries later (which included two modestly priced bottles of wine) and hours and hours of skimming, whipping, baking, and madly stirring, they walked in to our dinner party. It was a complete success, and they seemed pleased with the food and the ambience. Still, at the end of the night, our dinner party had set us back just under $100, two weeks worth of groceries for us. A dinner for four for

$100 is certainly affordable if everyone pays for themselves, but when one couple or person hosts, that means shouldering the expense.

So what is the solution? If a dinner party is expensive, and dining out in a large group (prone to unfair bill-splitting) is also prohibitively pricey, than what is an Urban Girl to do?

Ever inventive, ever ingenious, the Urban Girl has her escape route, her secret weapon, her saving solution.

She has tricks up her sleeve to host her friends without clearing out her bank account; she relishes having people over, borrowing chairs from neighbors' apartments, using every single last bowl and plate and fork she has in her cabinets, trying out new dishes on her unsuspecting buddies, giggling her way through cleaning up with one or two lingering friends. The Urban Girl turns every occasion into an event, every get-together into a bonanza.

First of all, she sets a menu filled with dishes that are surprisingly low-cost. She likes to think of them as her secret stunners. These dishes wow guests so much they will never know how cheap and easy they were. Try some of these tricks and watch your friends' jaws drop. Be ready to jot down your delicious recipes for friends.

Fish stew

Go to the supermarket and buy the cheapest fish available, a cusk or pollock or ocean catfish.

In a large saucepan, make a nice tomato sauce, simmering whole tomatoes, basil, oregano, tomato paste, and oil.

Add a couple bottles of clam juice, and a little handful of fresh thyme and sliced orange. Simmer for about five minutes.

Add the fish, and simmer for about one more minute. It's ready to serve.

Having a big party? Just buy more ingredients.

Deviled eggs

Deviled eggs are such a delight; they're the kind of dish that most people know is sort of gross, but still secretly enjoy. (Really, people might be wary to admit it, but just watch 'em dive for the eggs!)

Simply hard boil eggs (see below).

Remove shell immediately after boiling. Cut eggs down the center, separate out the yolk from the whites, which you place cut side up on a platter.

In a small bowl, mush up the yolks with a fork and add mayonnaise, mustard, and salt to taste. Use a small teaspoon to refill the egg whites with the yolk mixture.

Sprinkle with chopped chives or paprika. Serve with a smile.

Mint juleps

These are paired wonderfully with deviled eggs, for a sort of silly trailer trash vibe.

The night before, fill a large glass jar or measuring cup with bourbon and a handful of mint leaves. Chill overnight.

The next morning, remove the mint and add a few teaspoons of confectioners sugar, to taste.

Fill a lowball glass with crushed ice, and ¾ full of the mint-infused bourbon. Add a few teaspoons of water, run a lemon rind around the rim of the glass, and drop it in.

Final touch: add a mint sprig to the glass.

Go easy. These puppies are strong!

Potato salad

Potato salad is another dish that is an immediate crowd pleaser, evoking a summer picnic.

Take red new potatoes, boil them, and cut them up into quarters.

Add mayonnaise (and mustard if you like) and a couple teaspoons of whole milk yogurt, which you can cut with a teaspoon or two of sour cream.

best hard-boiled eggs

Sure, anyone can hard boil an egg, but the Urban Girl likes to do it just so. Here's how:

- Bring a pot of water to a fast boil, turn it down slightly so the boil is moderate.
- With a slotted spoon, gently place room temperature eggs in the water. Leave in boiling water for **ten minutes exactly**.
- Remove and plunge in ice water bath.

Add a tablespoon each of butter and vinegar.

Chop up chives and sprinkle over potatoes.

Stir it all up and serve.

Bean salad

This dish is one of my favorites because it can be as embellished or as simple as you like, depending on what you scavenge in your kitchen.

In one big serving bowl, combine canellini, canned tuna, fresh basil, and halved cherry tomatoes.

Generously douse with your best olive oil, sprinkle with salt and pepper.

Add in a tiny dash of balsamic vinegar.

Slice up a fresh ciabatta, or baguette, and serve.

Roast chicken

This dish is great for serving a large group, especially if you buy one whole chicken that the deli or grocery store has already cut up rather than pricier boneless, skinless breasts or tenders. (When buying your chicken, consider that each person will consume one pound of chicken.)

Rub the chicken with a lemon half.

Sprinkle with salt and pepper.

Add on any spices you might like, such as tarragon or rosemary.

Place in baking dish with peeled chopped onion, 3–4 cloves of garlic, and two tablespoons of melted butter.

Roast at 400 degrees for twenty minutes or until done, depending on thickness of pieces.

who knew?

Like a roast ham, some dishes are inevitably festive. Borrow a fondue pot and gather friends. Fight each other off with the fun tongs for the last slice of apple to dip in the warm, silky chocolate.

CO-OP DINNERS

You share embarrassing stories; you share clothes; you (shhh) sometimes share makeup. So why should cooking for your friends be a solo endeavor? We're still at an age when enlisting friends to help out isn't only kosher, it's expected.

Potlucks

You may be having ten people over for dinner, but enlist the fine art of delegating to share the labor of love. You are in charge of the main course; everyone else can handle a few salads, cornbread, desserts, and side dishes.

BYO...BBQs

Whether it's a veggie burger, a six-pack of beer, or kabobs, fill your hibachi with goodies from all attendees. You supply the coals, the Coleman, and the patch of green, along with a few patties and dogs to get the party started. Tell your friends to bring whatever they'd most enjoy eating. Put on a fun poufy BBQ hat to inspire your grilling prowess.

Cooking clubs

Sandra, a clothing buyer at a skateboarding company in New York, has a cooking club. She gets together with three close friends once a week.

who knew?

When searching for the perfect dessert recipe, think cupcakes. They're fun in a kitschy way, they're *cheap*, and they're easier than baking a whole cake or pie. Best of all, you won't need to wash plates and forks. The little suckers are perfect for popping straight into the mouth after unwrapping.

TIP: dinner party maxims

Enlist friends to help. When someone offers to bring something, they really would like to contribute. Let them. You are not Superwoman and Martha Stewart in one.

Focus on presentation. If you don't have killer plateware, work what you have. Arrange fish on a bed of lentils. Drizzle sauces in an impressive zigzag. Always use garnishes to add complementary colors.

Never apologize. If your soufflé falls, present it in nice bowls with a smile and flourish, and pronounce it "pudding." No one will notice, and if they do, they certainly won't say anything.

Instead of going out, they make each other dinner. Once a month, it's her turn. Each girl has her signature dish, whether it's stuffed shells or lasagna with a side of corn on the cob. Often, they'll find inspiration on the Food Network and divvy up the tasks. Everyone helps out. When they want to hang out with other people, they just invite them over to join them. Flip through *The Cooking Club Cookbook* for inspiration and ideas about what recipes are good to tackle *en masse*.

WEAR
section four

chapter twelve

the urban girl's look

"We are not looking for endless variety—we are looking for fashion."

—Diana Vreeland,
former editor in chief of *Vogue* and
fashion editor of *Harper's Bazaar*

from the afternoon you were caught red-handed in your mother's closet with a fistful of jewelry, clunking around in her high heels, with bright pink lipstick smeared across your cheeks, life as you know it has been a continuous process of discovering who you are. Glam or goth? Ghetto-fabulous or genteel? Who do you want to be today?

In high school, you experimented with a series of looks; knee-high boots one day, sneakers the next. Black nail polish one day, blue eye shadow the next. With a new hemline or headscarf, you were transformed from Debbie Harry to Lauryn Hill. But while changing it up on a daily basis may have had appeal while you were still in the research and development phase of your fashionable formation, for the cost-conscious Urban Girl, streamlining is a bottom-line necessity.

If everything up until now has been research, you're now ready for your unveiling. You've figured out your winning formula, your perfect hemline length, your tried-and-true color combinations.

Part of being an Urban Girl is having a well-defined sense of style, a refined, distinct look, and a smartly assembled wardrobe that works for you. A complete repertoire of clothes all in the same style gives you many options; you have ready-to-wear ensembles, and best of all, you have a slew of ideas. Things *go with each other*. And you can get out the door fast!

With your look all set, with a closet full of complementary clothes, the style mistakes you stumbled through while growing up—from tugging on too-tight skirts or drowning in diaper pants—are as far gone as acne and bad boyfriends. Ta-ta...and good riddance!

So, what is your look? Are you more Hyannis or Hamptons? Do you gravitate more toward pink or black? Flats or pumps? Style Network or CNN? The following breakdown will help you establish the look that's right for you.

Classic Carrie

Who is she? Preppy professional
What does she read? Anything Eloise, all Fitzgerald, and a dash of Foucault
Boys she's drawn to? Tortoiseshell Tad and Corduroy Chip

VIP (very important piece)? Crisp, collared shirts
Favorite color? White
Style icon? Kate Spade, Gwyneth Paltrow, Penelope Cruz
Poison of choice? Chardonnay, champagne

Downtown Diane
Who is she? A graphic designer
What does she read? William Burroughs, horoscopes, and *Paper* magazine
Boys she's drawn to? Tattooed Tim and Scooter Sam
VIP (very important piece)? Leather pants
Favorite color? Hot pink
Style icon? Gwen Stefani, Tara Subkoff, Maggie Gyllenhaal
Poison of choice? Gimlets

Trendy Tina
Who is she? A magazine editor
What does she read? Every publication she can get her hands on, chick lit, and Katharine Graham's autobiography
Boys she's drawn to? Black-framed glasses Bo, Attitude-prone Allen
VIP (very important piece)? Black slingbacks, Prada anything
Favorite color? Black
Style icon? Anna Wintour
Poison of choice? Manhattan

Hip Helen
Who is she? An artist
What does she read? Palms, *Gourmet*, and Malcolm Gladwell
Boys she's drawn to? Out-of-reach Oscar, Writer William
VIP (very important piece)? The latest weathered denim
Favorite color? Gray
Style icon? Chloe Sevigny, Kate Hudson
Poison of choice? Slim cigs

Now that you've narrowed down your stylish inclinations by identifying with one persona, it's time to dig deep and decide what your fashion needs are. If every day is an occasion to slip into something more comfortable, then halter tops are probably not a key purchase to make. If dressing to the nines is a job requirement, then another pair of cool sneakers is an extra you might not want to indulge.

Now, there will be some ladies who operate on the fashion fringes. And for them, the rules are easy—and extreme. For example, any self-respecting vixen must have a blood-red lipstick, curled eyelashes, a pushup bra, and an assortment of suggestive thongs. No goth can get down and freaky without an eclectic and expansive array of black vinyl miniskirts and thigh-high plastic boots. And any self-respecting sporty type from Connecticut simply selects the latest Lilly Pulitzer pastels, a good facial moisturizer, and the kicker: stark-white tennies.

But for girls like us, neither *out there* nor beyond the city limits, putting together a satisfyingly complete but still small, well-thought-out wardrobe can be a little trickier. Sift through everyone's Dos, Don'ts, and Nevers!, and you'll soon be swimming in a pile of clothes, tearing your hair out, crying, "Why me?"

So spare yourself. The lists vary, and more often than not, the rules don't really apply. For Urban Girls, it's all about pulling it off with panache, anyway. Take Kate, a stylish boutique owner in Boston's Beacon Hill. She is never without a pair of clogs, which allow her to stay on her feet all day without forming blisters or back pain. She buys them at a nurse's outfitter shop and pairs them with anything and everything: jeans, frilly skirts. For Kate, clogs are key.

Above all, Urban Girls are realistic, flexible, and out to look terrific.

THE BOTTOM LINE:
ON NOT GETTING HEMMED IN

Let's face it. Everyone's schedule varies, and those of us fortunate enough not to have to toil away under fluorescent lights and the warm glow of a computer screen have different needs than the nine-to-fiver clocking in and out by the tick of industrial clocks. Everyone has different requirements for a functional wardrobe that is both professionally appropriate and looks great.

On any given day in New York, Sarah, an architecture book editor and freelance photographer, must run from the office to the darkroom, wearing clothes that are both nice and casual enough that a little spray from developing solution wouldn't be the end of the world. In Washington, D.C., Juliet races from the jewelry studio to graduate seminars on psychology, alternating clothes dirty enough to spill polish on and nice enough to score points with her professor. In Boston, Ellie, a filmmaker, needs loungey, comfortable writing clothes, as well as power show-me-the-money ensembles worthy of convincing foundations to fund her work.

Me? Well, I often find myself running from intimate and prolonged encounters with my keyboard to gallery openings; from meetings with editors to the gym; from interviewing a famous person to dinner downtown with friends, which turns into a night of dancing. And throughout it all, one thing is certain: I would never be caught dead in a little black dress at *any* one of those events. I'm not a girl who wears pearls; I think I own a little black dress, but chances are at the moment it's crumpled at the bottom of my closet. I prefer using fashion to deliver a message, whether it's a frivolous fun little skirt or flashy red velvet pants, and the little black dress is merely a uniform, one that doesn't do much for this Urban Girl.

Every Urban Girl is a different person. We're real women with real jobs and real needs. So ditch the blanket statements about what every woman must have in order to be a Real Lady. Find your profile below and follow suit.

Profile I: Graduate Student

Fashion identity: Hip Helen

Typical day: The Graduate Student wakes up around 10 or 11 A.M., rolls out of bed, and lunges straight for the coffeemaker. A few cups later, she heads off to lead an undergraduate section, where she must look at least a *little* nicer than her mussed up, track-suit outfitted, ponytail-sporting, slouching students. After lunch, she meets with her doctoral advisor to discuss progress (or lack thereof) on her four hundred-page tome on post-post-post-feminism. Later on, the Graduate Student dives into a stack of books in a secluded corner of the library, where she sequesters herself with her fourth cup of coffee of the day and stashes her cell phone (on vibrate) in the pocket of her pants, just in case the professor calls. The Graduate Student stumbles out a little after midnight and makes her way to a much-needed date with friends at a local watering hole.

Needs: Professional, scholarly, comfortable, *dirt cheap*

Essential items, a partial list:

- **A black blazer.** The Graduate Student can throw a well-cut blazer over just about anything to transition from scrappy bookworm to Large-and-In-Charge teacher.
- **Thin black wool pants.** A good, thin wool can work well in summer as well as winter, when the pants can be bolstered by a pair of thick tights or leggings.
- **Turtleneck sweaters in dark colors.** Everything must be dark to mask dirt from *loooong* trips between visits to the laundromat. A turtleneck conveys a certain dark, brooding, Truffaut-loving, chain-smoking image for the serious types while also being just plain comfortable. A slouchy turtleneck with a wide cowl neck can turn the look into downtown chic.
- **A pair of wedge loafers.** A little lift combined with a comfortable slip-on loafer works well with jeans and skirts. And there's no need to waste precious time lacing up pesky shoes or zipping up high boots.
- **Good thick-frame iconic glasses.** They are the footnote that pulls the whole look together, the postscript that answers all the remaining questions, the glue that leaves the final impression. But choosing the right density is key. Think Ashleigh Banfield for bold faces.

Graduate Student style icons: Amanda Peet, Natalie Portman, Ali McGraw in *Love Story*

Profile II: The Office Worker

Fashion identity: Classic Carrie

Typical day: The Office Worker keeps a strict, regimented nine to five or six P.M. schedule. Some days, however, it's more like nine to eight, so she must be flexible.

The Office Worker groans into her pillow as the alarm blares far too early at 7:30 A.M. She hops in the shower and selects an ensemble for work. Her shoes must be comfortable enough that she can manage the walk to the subway, but far from drab. White tennies over tights are not an option here. *Don't even think about it.* She heads to work, where she alternates between emailing friends, taking calls, running back and forth to the printer (while she prints out resumes to send out to find a better job, *shhh*) and going to "meetings" where she must seem professional, demure, driven, and obsequious, all at once. The OW finally leaves the warm hue of florescent lights for the dark streets, meeting up with friends for cocktails to tie one on and "take the edge off."

Needs: Transitional, corporate with edge, aspiringly ambitious, *dirt cheap*

Essential items:

- **Low slingbacks.** The OW must be able to pull off functional and fashionable, which will be possible with a low, wide heel.
- **A colored cardigan.** A knit sweater in a soft angora or merino wool can both dress up pants or a skirt and cover up the sexy tank for later.
- **A black A-line skirt.** The crisp, straight line of this skirt will be both comfortable and appropriate.
- **Button down shirts.** A hint of stretch and a wide array of bright colors, from pink to baby blue, will pair well with everything else in black.

Office Worker style icons: The girls in *The Last Days of Disco*, Parker Posey in *Clock Watchers*

Profile III: Artist

Fashion identity: Downtown Diane

Typical day: To assume that the artist has a typical day would be, like, *so* out of character. The artist has only one agenda, which is to create. And getting boxed into a schedule of any kind is not conducive to the whir of genius swirling around in the brain that sits somewhere under those utterly ironic pigtail braids. However, the artist does have a certain mix of activities that make up her day. Somewhere amid the twenty-four hours, she will do some, if not all, of these activities: brood on the couch about how everything she creates is crap; worry about money; head to her studio and paint/write poems/develop photos/throw pots/edit film/design clothes; go to the neighborhood café and brood some more; have drinks with other artist friends and come up with genius ideas, gesticulating wildly; write letters/meet with people who can provide money to fund the continuation of said daily regimen.

Needs: Iconic, original, expendable, *dirt cheap*

Essential items:

- **Clunky clogs.** When the artist is ready to create (a rare, beautiful moment), she must have shoes that allow her to forget that she is standing, and get fully immersed in her reverie of artistic production.
- **Overalls.** It may be a fashion cliché, but there's something to throwing on an oversized pair of mussed up overalls—preferably Ben Davis, in stripes—that's inherently conducive to creating.
- **Head wraps.** A scarf, a hair tie, whatever the weapon, this touch provides a dual purpose of creating an arty look and keeping those damn wisps out of the artist's peepers.
- **Black.** It doesn't matter what the item is, as long as it is in black. It adds to the brooding, stormy look.

Artist style icons: Edie Sedgwick, Jade Jagger

Profile IV: Service Employee (museum ticket taker, movie theater employee, creator of lattes extraordinaire, chef)

Fashion identity: Trendy Tina

Typical day: The SE has more unpredictable clothing needs, depending on her job. She must look both presentable and maintain her own image. The SE is irreverent and, for the most part, responsible. She arrives at work (*oops!*) a few minutes late and races to her post. She tries desperately to recite the phrase "the customer is always right," while knowing the opposite is more often than not true. Over the course of the next eight hours—minus her thirty-minute break for lunch and her fifteen-minute "coffee break"—she manages to spill on herself, trip, and drop something on her foot. No matter the position the SE has, one thing is most likely true: she is both on her feet and often highly visible. Post-clocking out, the SE races to meet up with friends where she collapses into a little ball of exhaustion over a shot of whiskey. *Sigh*.

Needs: Respectable, relaxing, comfortable, *dirt cheap*

Essential items:

- **Funky sweaters.** The SE needs to work within the boundaries of what is appropriate while also adding her own flair. Sweaters in wild colors or cuts make her both distinctive and down with the decorum.
- **Three-quarter length T-shirts.** With a touch of spandex and a boat or crew neck, these shirts can be paired with nice pants to be great-looking without being too fancy.
- **Jeans.** A great pair of jeans with no wild, distressed lines or manufactured holes can be dressed up or down, depending on the SE's position.
- **Black pants.** The black hides the spills, while also flattering the SE's figure. What more can she ask for in a piece of clothing?

Service Employee style icons: Jennifer Aniston, Winona Ryder in *Reality Bites*

Profile V: Unemployed (i.e., Temporarily Between Jobs)

Fashion identity: Any of the above, depending on who she's meeting that day

Typical day: The TBJ must not wallow in a self-flagellating state of sloth. She must wake, dress, and create a dense schedule of activities to launch herself into a wonderful routine. When the TBJ is not madly surfing the Web for fabulous jobs or meeting with contacts to feel out possible positions, she must take it upon herself to exercise, read, and cook. Thus, the TBJ will rise at a respectable hour, change immediately out of her PJs into an outfit that says, "I'm a winner," rather than "Why would anyone hire me?" The TBJ will alternate between primping and fine-tuning her resume, with which she will blanket the town. When leaving her apartment, the TBJ will look both casual and put together, far from corporate, but miles away from don't-give-a-damn.

Needs: Inspirational, confident, turned-out, *dirt cheap*

Essential items:

- **Cool sneakers.** Call them trainers, call them sneaks, call them running shoes—whatever. The point is the TBJ should own at least one pair of Pumas, Adidas, or Jack Purcells in crisp white or funky colors to add a little spunky flava.
- **Brushed twill black pants.** The fabric will hang loose and soft and can transition easily from the couch to a lunch meeting.
- **A chic suit.** The TBJ must be ready at any moment to throw on the monkey suit and to sell herself for the million bucks that she's worth. When in doubt, the TBJ would do best pairing the jacket with a skirt rather than pants.
- **Black button-down shirt.** Versatility is quite important for the TBJ. This item can be thrown on over just about anything and pull off chic casual or—if the occasion calls for it—sexy downtown Do Me.

TBJ Style Icons: Janeane Garofalo, Natasha Lyonne

A LOOK OF HER OWN

Whether she's the Downtown Diane or the Trendy Tina, the Urban Girl has her very own distinctive look. Her line of work helps orient her in what her clothing needs are, what her essential items must be, whether it's the demure turtleneck or the sexpot pushup bra. Sure, this is good for one's self-image, but more importantly, it's essential in streamlining your clothing expenses.

If you really have a handle on your style, you can head straight for the items that multitask. The black pencil skirt that is half of a suit also works with a halter top on steamy summer nights. All the best style icons have their look down. Think of Kate Spade, who has her very own distinctive retro, pulled-together, clean-lined aesthetic. Or Jackie O, who was the consummate uptown lady with designer denim and Halston sweaters.

To get started, simply open those eyes and look around. Consider your head one big filing cabinet; fill it with clippings, images, and anecdotes. Tear pages from magazines, clip newspaper articles, tape your favorite style show on E!.

Refining your look is your post-grad thesis in You, your final project. As with any major task, you can start your research by reading. Use your senses: sight, smell, touch, and sound. See something on the street? Take a mental note. Tune in to what's around you.

Malls and shopping districts aren't the only place where the Urban Girl can conduct research. Ever on the quest to see it all, she turns her eagle eye on every source of information, from the streets to her favorite novel to the corner newsstand. The resources are everywhere. *Open your eyes*.

Think literature

From an Evelyn Waugh novel to a chick lit treatment such as Candace Bushnell's *Four Blondes*, authors can instruct on more than just painting an accurate portrait of a character.

For example, Valerie Steiker's delightful and mature memoir of her iconic mother, *The Leopard Hat*, is a veritable ode to fashion ideas. Steiker's mother was a firecracker Belgian who started trends without even trying. One time, a bee sting left a swollen mark on her upper arm. To hide the imposing lump, she cinched a scarf on her arm. It was a fashion band-aid she threw together on impulse without a second thought. But apparently, it had what Malcolm Gladwell would call "stickiness." By the next day, the arm scarf was *the* look at the resort town she was visiting. The arm scarf, sort of a new take on the Punky Brewster leg scarf. Hey, why not try it?

Think newsstands

Magazines are a primary source for scoping out great fashion. And every girl has her poison. Some only read glossies from across the pond *(e.g.; British Vogue, French Vogue, The Face)*. Others religiously riffle through odes to shopping produced on these shores, like *Lucky*, the Condé Nast publication devoted exclusively to shopping. But it's also worth noting that sometimes inspiration can come from the most unlikely source. *National Geographic Adventure*: hell-ooo Safari Style. *New Yorker*: Intellectual Ingénue; *The Source*: wassup, Hip Hop Mama.

Truly, magazine fashion spreads, articles about trends, and even advertisements are chock full of interesting images. A layout on wild women of the Maldives isn't only eye candy, though. You can peruse the captions to see the what, where, and how much. Consider it a sort of armchair shopping. Find out just how ridiculously high-priced those tan khaki shorts are. And then do a dance of joy when you find them for a price you can actually afford.

Reading through everything you can get your hands on may not exactly sound like a way to keep that shoestring budget. In fact, it's a far from frugal affair, you might think. $3+$2.75+$4, etc., every month? But who says you have to buy the publications? While some newsstands are run by hysterical hands-on proprietors *(are you gonna buy that?)*, big bookstores, small delis, and grocery stores all stock the glossy goodies. Throw some gum in your basket and flip away.

Think catalogs

Even the most unlikely catalog can be a font of ideas. Whether the topic is gardening or bras, you can become a well-informed expert about various styles simply from opening your mailbox. Take *Martha by Mail*. Here, amid spreads about tulip seeds and post-weeding hand lotion, one can find terrific ideas and concepts for reviving old clothes.

After reading through the catalog recently, I sewed buttons back on a black raincoat I bought in Italy a few years ago that had been unwearable for the past year without its buttons. I scrubbed a stain off of a pair of thin gray pants. I bought a lint brush and attacked a velvet blazer.

And in that hour, my closet gained about $300 in value since I could finally wear the items whose cleaning up I had prolonged. Martha didn't even need to tell me how to do it; I just had to see some inspiringly stylized images to get cracking in my closet.

Think Internet

Some of the best places to find information these days are obviously on the Internet. But you need to know where to look. Start out your quest to enrich your fashion sense by simply turning on your computer and heading to fashion message boards.

The best message boards will convey the most up-to-date fashion sensibilities. People often poll each other about what goes with what. Girls gather opinions on who else loves the latest looks from Dolce & Gabbana. You can find answers to every conceivable fashion question, ("Can I wear yellow with orange?" and "Where can I find red tights?")

some great sites with forums and fashion inspiration:

www.style.com   www.lucky.com
www.instyle.com   www.mightyflirt.com
www.katespade.com   www.eluxury.com

weeding in your closet

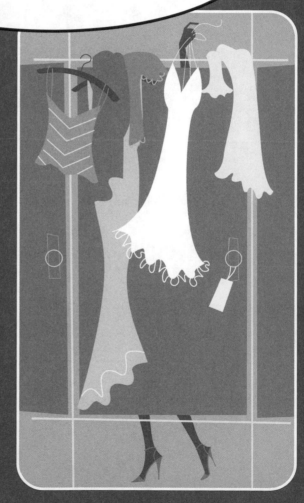

"Really take a good look at what you have. When I have a great pair of pants that fit my butt really well, I don't do away with them! I take them to the tailor and get them cuffed."

—Elisabeth Filarski, host of Style Network's *The Look for Less* and former competitor on *Survivor Australia*

before heading off to shop with a credit card and a head bursting with big ideas, you must decide what you need. Shopping on whimsy, without a list, is a recipe for trouble. *Oooh! I'll have one of those, and one of those.* Danger! One month later, you get your bill and have a heart attack. Avoid the palpitations by being informed about what you already have and what you need.

Chances are, your closet is filled with finds you've forgotten about. And if it isn't, those hangers and duds are just taking up precious space in your cozy (read: cramped) pad.

What do you already have that you're forgetting?

Every so often, you tear open that closet door and sigh in defeat. *I'm sooo sick of my clothes!* It feels like you wear the same thing...every...single...day. That's because you do. But underneath the well-worn layer of your favorite jeans, your perfect black blouse, and your everyday tank is a wealth of other options. Dig deep.

It may be time for a Closet Purge. To mine the forgotten riches, pull every single item out of your closet as needed (once or twice a year), and lay them all on your bed in piles. Divide into three separate stacks: Essential Everyday; Special Occasion; and Can't Remember *For the Life of Me* the Last Time I Wore It. Be ruthless in deciding which pieces go in which piles. And most importantly, be honest with yourself.

Ditch the nostalgia and toss anything that you haven't touched in at least one year.

Your ex-boyfriend's holey rugby shirt. The dress you were wearing when you got your first job. Your mom's sweater from England circa 1952. Your formerly favorite jeans that have a conspicuous hole between the legs.

Get real. You are not going to wear these pieces any time soon. And your closet, stuffed to the gills with never-worn clothes, is the worse for them. By cramming them in, your truly precious wares are getting all wrinkled and smushed. If you absolutely must keep your memory-laden clothes, put them in a box with your other mementos you don't plan on putting on: a photo album, a freshman year mix tape.

Can you do anything to give your borderline clothes a face lift?

Of course, there will be items in the mix that are in desperate need of TLC. A coat missing a button, a sweater with a hole in the armpit, jeans with a stain you tried to rub out with water and a paper towel. Standing there amid the stack of second-rate items, you may be tempted to toss anything that isn't in perfect condition. Avoid the impulse, Urban Girl. With only a little time and some supplies, you can reinvigorate your flagging clothing fortune. All clothing items, however fabulous, will go through down periods, from wrinkles to spots. Your wardrobe is For Better or For Worse: stick with it, put in some work, and turn the fortune around.

Buttons. If you're missing a button on a blouse and tossed the extra button that came with it, just replace all of them. Better yet, if you have a sweater or a jacket that's great-looking except for cheap buttons, invest in the best, replace them, and increase the value of your clothes.

Holes. As long as it's on a seam, a hole is an easy fix. Just be sure to use the same color thread as is used in the rest of the garment.

Stains. See chapter 14. The worst thing you can do with a stain is cry, give up, and let it sit. Give it your informed all, trying every concoction known to man.

How much do you really need? When is more not necessarily better?

Once you've sorted through the contents of your closet, prepared bags to be taken to Goodwill, and made your peace with the stack doomed for donation, it's time to figure out where the holes are in your wardrobe. You know what you have, but what do you need?

Divide and conquer.

Count up every pair of jeans, every nice T-shirt, every skirt, every boot. And then think about what your wardrobe needs are. If your lifestyle calls for chic boots every day, maybe that one scuffed pair isn't enough. If your job calls for suits, having yet another pair of distressed denim, which you can wear Saturday and Sunday, may be a bit excessive.

Be honest with yourself and make a list.

This is one of those unusual times when more may not be better. So what are reasonable measures? An Urban Girl, whatever her line of work and whatever her line of play, should have certain things in her closet in certain numbers. Each should fit perfectly, make the Girl feel like a Queen, and go with the majority of everything else in her closet.

Jeans: 2 to 4 pair
Slacks: 5 pair summer, 5 pair winter
Skirts: 5 in a variety of lengths, depending
  on the shape of the Urban Girl's legs
Dresses: 4
Blouses: 6 to 10
Nice T-shirts: 10
Tank tops: 10
Long-sleeved shirts: 6 to 8
Sweaters: 10
Shoes: ?? (as many as you can afford)

General rules for wardrobe quantity

You can get away with having fewer bottoms if you have many tops. If you can change your shirt, you can wear the same pair of pants multiple times in a week, as long as they don't have a crazy, recognizable pattern on them like vertical stripes or polka dots.

Build from the bottom up. Shoes, then pants, then shirt, then accents, like scarves or belts.

Invest in items that can multitask, like a dress that can be a skirt when you throw on a cute cardigan.

Whether unemployed, a slave to an executive, or working toward a degree, all girls will need a few signature pieces in their wardrobe repertoires. They will be stashed away at the back of the closet, ready for the Big Unveiling. Combined with the basics above, the meat and potatoes, these pieces will complete the picture. The Urban Girl will have it all covered: from the fancy fêtes to the Monday morning meetings to the Sunday afternoon curling up on the couch session.

Spice it up

As with any dish, whipping up a simple bowl of chicken stock won't satisfy anyone except only those ladies with the most bland palate. Even when you add in your meat and potatoes, it's still a bowl of boring stew. Throw in some garlic, toss in some Cajun spices already!

Any self-respecting Urban Girl will take the basics and embellish, arranging them delicately and gorgeously on the plate. She must season the style stew a bit. Whatever your profile, and whatever basics you choose, a few accents can take your basic wardrobe from staid and boring to *spicy. Olé!*

On a whim at a recent visit to Filene's Basement, I found a wide black belt by Nine West with a big silver loop and an angled slouch to it. I threw it around my waist, cinched it over my pants' belt loops, and decided it absolutely had to come home with me. The $20 price tag was, of course, a clincher. I wasn't sure how it would work, but I knew that even if it didn't, I wasn't taking too much of a risk.

Soon enough, I was throwing it on with anything. Over a pair of tight jeans on a night out to see some German electronic DJ; at work with a black miniskirt and a tan ribbed turtleneck sweater; paired with corduroys and

TIP: style signatures

- A perfect pair of black pants
- A suit that pulls off sexy and demure
- A perfect pair of jeans, weathered and distressed just like you like them
- A black V-neck sweater
- A black cardigan sweater
- A go-with-everything coat
- A carry-all leather shoulder bag

my hair pulled back tight on laundry day. The belt seemed to pull everything together. Without it, my outfits would have been simply jeans, a skirt, and cords. With it, there was some flair, some, well, *me*.

Sometimes, spice can seem daring and perhaps a little over-the-top. But an Urban Girl will always get respect for trying something new, digging deep into her repertoire and getting creative. Recently, I was out on a morning of shopping with Gigi Guerra, an editor for *Lucky* magazine, whose job it is to find the best stores in a city and tell readers where they can score the coolest clothes. After trolling through several stores, we collapsed into chairs at an outdoor café for lunch and proceeded to people-watch, scouting out interesting looks. When a woman walked by with two tube tops on, one on top, and the other wrapped tight around her thighs and bum—over a pair of jeans—we weren't the only table noting her stand-out style. Some people laughed, others leered. I asked Gigi what she thought.

"I salute her!" she concluded quickly and generously. "Good for her for trying something new." An Urban Girl isn't fearful of throwing two unlikely items together; she goes for it and tests out the waters. Even a tube top over the bum can get respect if you pull it off with conviction.

chapter fourteen

behind the seams

Your favorite low-slung pants lightly kiss the ground when you wear the wrong pair of shoes. Your new overpriced sweater just snagged on the corner of your desk drawer, leaving a string trailing off the sleeve. You just spilled some of your morning coffee on your pant leg. And your socks? Well, you should have trashed them three months ago. And that's just what you're wearing *today*.

It's enough to make even the most fabulous girl feel like a complete slob. Some days, after sewing buttons, discovering stains, and sadly trashing a formerly white tee, I feel like all I ever do is take care of my clothes.

"I spend so much money on dry cleaning," moans my friend Angela. Working in a small architectural firm in Cambridge, she doesn't have much to spare on having her pants neatly pressed and her shirts regularly laundered. It's a common conundrum for most style-conscious women: keeping clean.

And it's a hard expense to swallow. At the end of the day, the more meticulous you are, the less people will notice. The work is, well, behind the seams. Launder your weekly shirts? Be prepared to spend $50 a month. A monthly shoeshine for your favorite pair? Try $15. Tailor a new pair of pants? It can be up to $20. All together, you're looking at an annual expense of more than $1,000. Just so you don't look like a shlump!

For the cost-conscious, it might be hard to see the benefit of being attentive to those sweat stains, thinned-out soles, and dragging hems in the face of such a draw. But here's why maintenance pays:

Longer life spans

Regularly care for your wool sweaters and they'll last longer. If you tailor pants *before* they drag, you won't damage them to the point of their sad death. Susan Taylor, an Educator on Consumer and Family Economics with University of Illinois Extension, recommends remaining attentive to only a select number of pieces, like a pricey winter coat. "You end up saving money in the long run," she says, "If you have a $250 coat, you need to take care of it, otherwise you'll run into moth problems. I do spend a lot of money midseason taking care of coats so that they are clean in that respect."

Better appearance now

If you notice that stain, it's fairly likely your boss will, too...and your girl-friend, and your roommate. And you're not saying much about yourself if you walk around a mess of tatters, spills, and dragging shoe soles. Take care of your personal business and your style stock rises exponentially.

Amanda, 31, a reporter in New York, recalls her first job interview with an editor at the newspaper for which she now works. It took place on an unseasonably warm day in May. "The only nice clothes I had were these wool-lined pants and a suede jacket I bought at a thrift store in London," she remembers, with an amused smile. But Amanda shrugged off the improbable nature of the fabrics and did her best by making sure every-thing looked clean and unrumpled. She sweated her way through the inter-view and got the job! Who cares if it was wool; she handled herself coolly.

Peace of mind

Lisa, 27, a legal assistant in Denver, regularly plans out her outfits a night in advance. But the next morning at 6 A.M., as she pulls her pieces from the closet, Lisa is often greeted by the depressing sight of specks, loose strings, or gray ash marks from girlfriends' cigarettes. It's frustrating. It's costly. And it also throws her for a loop, causing a last-minute rethinking of what she wants to wear. Keeping your clothes clean helps you feel in control. A well-maintained wardrobe keeps you sane as well as stylish.

Nonetheless, you can look tidy and put together without having to clean out your bank account.

Dry cleaning vs. hand washing

Certainly, there are those who avoid DRY CLEAN ONLY tags like pegged pants or the plague. And there are those who buy them but ride the line between dirty and clean, waiting as long as possible before drop-offs at the dry cleaner. But there's no need to do either in your new budget-conscious mode.

First of all, if the tag says DRY CLEAN instead of DRY CLEAN ONLY, you're in luck. You can usually trust those wares to Woolite. Really. The Federal Trade Commission made it a law that a tag can say DRY CLEAN when it's also possible to wash. But if it says DRY CLEAN ONLY, that's the only course to clean. What that means is that labels aren't necessarily giving you all of the information.

"The truth is that many cashmere items can be washed safely at home," clarifies the FTC in its Care Labeling Act. "A label that says DRY CLEAN does not warn against washing and does not require proof that washing would harm the item."

That's good news to someone like Jane, a jewelry maker in Boston, who doesn't have a cent to spare in her budget for something as seemingly luxurious as dry cleaning. Over the course of the years, she's ruined a fair number of garments in figuring out more cost-friendly alternatives. And now she has it down pat. "I never take my clothes to the dry cleaners," she says. "I'm a huge fan of hand washing. Woolite is the greatest invention. I save tons of money every month."

Experts agree. Katherine Hatch, author of *Textile Science*, doesn't have one item in her closet that needs to be dry cleaned. "If I can't throw it in the washer and the dryer, it doesn't leave the store with me," she says.

Dry-Cleaning Dos and Don'ts

Silk: if it's not a bright garment, you're safe hand-washing it. But if it's a bright color, dry cleaning will prevent the color from running or fading.

100% cotton: any type of clothing that's all cotton can be hand washed.

Any sort of blend: if you have any combination of cotton, Lycra, or polyester, you're doomed to dry clean.

Wool sweaters: as long as it's only made up of one thread or material, you're safe to hand wash, but don't leave it soaking for more than a minute.

Home Dry Cleaning Kits

Over the past few years, a number of companies have introduced home dry cleaning systems. The kits, which run for around $10, include a spot stick, a dry cloth, and a bag. After pre-treating the clothes for stains, you can throw up to four items in the nylon bag with a dryer-activated solvent and toss them into the dryer for up to thirty minutes. And then you cross your fingers. If all goes well, the clothes will heat up enough in the bag that they'll activate the cloth, which will release a combination of steam, perfume, and an emulsifier.

University of Illinois's Taylor says the kits can be great for removing stale cigarette odor or generally freshening up in between irregular visits to the dry cleaner. "They're really freshening agents," adds Karen Koza, the director of marketing for the American Apparel and Footwear Association. The real deal, she stresses, is necessary to remove hidden dirt specks and persistent scents. A few of the options:

- Custom Cleaner, made by Dial
- FreshCare, made by Clorox
- Dryel, made by Procter & Gamble

STAIN REMOVAL

Some of us cannot be trusted with food, drink, pens, or anything that could leave a trace. Within minutes, there's a colorful remnant on your lap, your sleeve, your French cuff. Sure, it's only a dribble, but it screams *slob*.

Kerry, 26, a waitress cum singer in Boston, has one way to deal with the mess: "I don't dare wear white," she explains. But there's no need to don bibs or all-black wardrobes all the time. And don't resign yourself to turning around and heading straight to the dry cleaners. Instead, try the supermarket. There, you'll find items to stock your own home care cleaning system. And the big bottles will have enough to take care of tomorrow's inevitable drools, spills, and slips, too.

Just make sure to tend to your mess right away. "With stains, the sooner you get to them the better off you're going to be," notes Taylor. "If you're at a dinner party and something happens, you can wait a little time, but try to deal with it that evening."

No matter the source of the stain, Taylor says your chances of salvaging your favorite shirt come closer to 100 percent if you catch it right away. And don't be afraid to take a few stabs at your stain removal techniques.

Ingredients and instructions for your supermarket stain removal kit

- **Club soda**—for white wine
  Dab on gently and let sit.
- **Salt**—for red wine
  Immediately coat with salt and let it soak up the moisture. Rinse with cold water.
- **White vinegar**—for pit perspiration
  Douse discolored sections with warm vinegar, let sit, and wash thoroughly in hot water.
- **Salad oil**—for lipstick
  Rub conservatively on color and let sit before laundering.
- **Hairspray**—for pen ink
  Hold garment in front of a towel, spritz stain from behind, let seep through and sit before washing.

IRONING OUT THE WRINKLES

It always seems like the most necessary purchase: an iron and one of those portable boards to stash in the closet. After all, a girl can't be without an iron, right? But then it sits there, silently chiding while you inspect yourself in the full-length mirror, negotiating with yourself about whether your wrinkled pants can pass...and the precious preparty minutes tick by.

TIP: fabric washing rules 101

Not sure how to care for your pieces? Consult this crib sheet:

Cotton	Machine wash gentle, temp varies according to color
Linen	Machine wash gentle in cold or warm (hot makes it shrink)
Nylon	Wash separately
Silk	Handwash in cold water
Wool	Handwash inside out in warm or cold water and dry flat

"I have this shirt that I can't even wear," moans Lisa. "I put it on for five minutes and I look like I just rolled out of bed. I can iron, I can not iron—it doesn't matter. I always look the *worst*."

For some, a few quick swipes with the neglected domestic appliance are far from a hateful prospect. But then again, an easier solution would be to stock your closet with fabrics that hold their shape. Two of the best wares for ironing avoidance:

Denim

It's not only fashionably convenient, these days there are no rules regarding denim. (*Denim on denim? Go for it!*) But the durable fabric also happens to be a low-maintenance girl's dream come true. Darker denim not only deceptively hides stains, the thicker fabric hardly wrinkles. Just try....

who knew?

Your favorite thing about sending your pants to the dry cleaners is that they come back with those expertly crisp creases. Achieve the smart-looking line at home by folding waxed paper where you want the crease to hold and ironing over the paper. A little melted wax will maintain the crease.

Synthetic stretchy fabrics

You may have teased your mom for her love of Lycra, but there was certainly something to it. "Stretch is great in the respect that in the interim between dry cleanings, it does take care of itself better," notes Karen Koza, the director of marketing at the American Apparel and Footwear Association. "It doesn't wrinkle as easily, and it retains its shape." Look for blends of polyester and cotton, triacetates, and acrylic.

LAUNDRY MISHAPS AND SAVING SOLUTIONS

You're so *good*. You do your laundry every week, you hand wash when it says to, you separate whites from colors, you darn, you attend to spills immediately. But still your clothes fade, your favorite sweater pills, and your jeans shrink so much you're embarrassed to wear them out of the house. *It's not fair*, you moan. Sure, you could whine and whimper. Or you could march out and replace your pricey wardrobe every six months. But why? Here's how to avoid the angst and save your sanity, your money, and your clothes.

Pilling

Those pesky nubs of fabric sprout up when a garment rubs up against itself, breaking fibers, which gather into tiny lumps called "pills." Remove the unsightly balls by pulling the piece of clothing taut over a curved surface and carefully cutting off the pills with scissors or a safety razor. Minimize pill growth in the future by washing pill-prone clothes inside out and removing them from the dryer as soon as it stops spinning.

Shrinkage

For garments known to lose an inch or two in the wash, such as jeans, cords, and cotton shirts, turn them inside out before washing them and only dry them to just about 90 percent complete. You'll know they're done when everything is dry except for the slightly damp seams. Additionally, Diana, a saleswoman at Diesel in Georgetown, once advised me to hold off on washing my jeans until absolutely necessary. "I haven't washed these," she exclaims, pointing down to her distressed hip-hugging jeans, "in four months!" Some salespeople are even more cautious. Diana's coworker Mark shakes his head, chiding that true denim devotees shouldn't even tempt fate with the dryer at all. I generally wait four to six months in between washing my jeans, to prevent fading. To ensure that your denim doesn't lose its shape during the six month gap in washings, buy jeans with a small amount of stretch in them. Also, a regular spritz of Febreze will remove any cosmetic odors.

Bleeding colors

Thrift or laziness may lead you to throw caution to the wind and dump all of your various clothing items into one washer. But when your white tees come out with pink spots, you learn fast. For slight color spots on white items, pour a quarter cup of lemon juice or dishwashing detergent in the wash next time and line dry in the sun. To keep your colorful clothes from running, prewash the fabric in water doused generously with salt or vinegar, which holds in color. If the run has already happened, products like Rit dye or Retayne, available at most supermarkets, can remove color runs.

Static

On my way to a recent meeting with my editor at *Glamour* magazine, I realized my skirt's slit was creeping up the back of my leg, exposing more upper thigh than is cute at a 3:30 daytime meeting. *Ahhh!* The risqué cut just would not do in the impeccably fashionable Condé Nast building. With only an hour to spare, I ducked into a Starbucks bathroom, pulled out some nail clippers from my bag, and made some snips to the lining, which (thank God) eliminated the terrible tug.

Prevent static cling by pouring a cup of white vinegar into the washer's final rinse cycle. If your clothes still come out of the dryer clinging to each other—and you—rub them all over with a wire clothes hanger, which should diffuse the electric charge.

Lint removal

Even when your clothes come out clean and unscathed, your dark-colored wares are often decorated with little bits of colorful fuzz. Pat the adhesive strip of a Fed Ex envelope over your linty garment. The unsightly fuzz will attach to the sticky substance.

who knew?

If your buttons are prone to pop off, dab a little clear nail polish on the center, where the thread is. As it dries, it will harden and hold.

BEST-CASE SCENARIO LIFESPAN

The seasonal ebb and flow of fashion dictum aside, your wares can last a long time if you give them the proper TLC. Here's an average **best-case-**

scenario lifespan for the garments of those not afraid to pick up a needle and thread, pull the Woolite out from under the sink, and attack those inevitable spills pronto.

The item	Life expectancy
Wool suit	Four years
Lightweight suit	Two years
Leather coat	Four to five years
Cloth coat	Three years
Cotton shirt	Two to three years
Sweater	Four years
Dress	Two years
Jeans	Four to five years

PIECEMEAL MAINTENANCE

When it comes to leather shoes and bags, it's an uphill battle to keep the wares looking *wow!* The leather cracks, the shoulder strap snaps, the shoes scuff. You can send them in for a full rehaul—and set yourself back a painful amount of cash—or you can have only the most crucial part fixed. A little-known secret is that many shops will do maintenance on only one segment, cutting potentially lofty costs.

For example:

Approximate Price	Saving service
$30	Have a leather bag or shoes redyed
$40	Have a bag's handle restitched
$60	Have a bag's handle replaced

Shining a light on shoes

Scuffed shoes scream out to be buffed. Don't drop $15 at a cobbler. Take matters in to your own hands in six simple steps:

1. Take off the laces.
2. Find a cotton cloth (an old T-shirt works great).
3. Wrap a small portion of cotton cloth around your pointer finger.

4. Buff away.
5. Let sit for ten minutes.
6. Use an old pair of pantyhose to shine them after the polish dries.

From *shmatteh* to sexy score

Stephanie Seeley, 29, a former assistant buyer at Louis Boston, an upscale clothing store, turns fashionably crafty when she finds herself sitting at home on evenings without a date. The pixie-like girl picks up an oversized Hanes men's white undershirt, puts it on, and tucks, pulls, and stretches it tight to fit herself snugly. She snips away excess material, cuts out angular necklines, and sews on everything from bits of lace curtain to discarded tablecloth, finishing up by embroidering the date of her productive stay-at-home evening on the back of the right shoulder. The result is part of a line she's started called Dateless T-shirts, which she now sells in shops in Boston, Los Angeles, San Francisco, and New York.

Following her lead can be easy. If all hope is truly lost in saving a piece of clothing, you can make the best of the worst by embarking on a clothing metamorphosis. Pick up a sewing guide book like Marjorie Baker's *New Clothes From Old* to assemble some basic knowledge. A few of the possibilities:

What was a	Can become
Dress	A pair of shorts, a shirt, a skirt
Skirt	A blouse, a head scarf
Long coat	A short jacket, a suit, a dress

chapter fifteen

shop 'n' save

"Good taste shouldn't have to cost anything extra."

—as quoted in the *New York Times* magazine by Mickey Drexler, former president of Gap, Inc.

now that you've done the work to decide what you want, what you have, and what you need, it's time to let the shopping games begin.

Before setting out, it's important to know just how many dollars you can drop. Debt is the Urban Girl's enemy, introducing stress-inducing wrinkles and too many nights at home trying to catch up with her out-of-control payments. It's also easily avoidable if you just keep an eye on the bottom line.

Start off on the right foot by always being aware of what you have and what is reasonable to spend. Somehow, with a shake of spice, a pinch of panache, and a dash of DIY confidence, an Urban Girl does it all with her small budget. And that includes shopping.

You're resourceful and intelligent; you're driven, and most importantly, you won't take no for an answer. You know there's no need to be frivolous in your quest for fabulousness. Chic comes cheap. All you have to do is set your limits, follow these four steps, and have faith.

STEP ONE:
COZY UP TO YOUR CALCULATOR

The answers are easy when it comes to rent. Someone dictates how much is appropriate to dole out each month in proportion to your income. When our parents were out there in their starter apartments, the number hovered around 25 to 30 percent. These days, it tends to be higher. Thank you, inflation. The rent ratio can creep up to 40 percent, and for some urbanites unwilling to sacrifice *location location location*, the number angles upward to 50.

Unfortunately, there's no similar set magic number for clothes. Some shopping experts have thrown around formulas in an attempt to add order to the madness, to provide guidance to us legions of cost-conscious clothes horses. We salute their efforts.

In her definitive book *Best Dressed*, shopping guru Suzy Gershman recommends allocating $\frac{1}{4}$ of your take-home pay for clothes shopping. But Gershman is speaking to an older audience with a far greater level of disposable income. For those of us on the upper scale—for whom rolling out of bed straight to the cool neighborhood hangout is more important than a classic Hermés scarf—¼ devoted to clothes may be too much.

Does the ¼ rule work for you? After setting aside ¼ for clothes plus ½ for rent, that leaves only ¼ for everything else—food, cocktails, gym membership, the occasional silly splurge, weekend jaunts to the country. However well-dressed I would like to be, shelling out ¼ of my slim income for clothes wouldn't be worth it for me since I could never leave the house and see the light of day! These days, ⅕ seems a much more reasonable amount to allocate for your clothing budget.

The ⅕ Clothing Budget

If your salary is:	Your ⅕ monthly clothing allowance is:
$20,000	$333
$25,000	$417
$30,000	$500
$35,000	$583
$40,000	$666

If ⅕ seems like too much, and you'd rather devote your cash to dining out, simply punch out a sum that is appropriate for you, either by ratio of monthly income or a set amount. After noting all your other necessary expenses, tally what's left and figure out how you want to spend it.

As my salary has changed year to year, sometimes for the better, more often for the worse, I sit down with a pen, paper, and a glass of wine to soften the blow. And then I figure out what my monthly allowance is (*cringe*). What I've learned is that whether that number is $200 or $2000 a month, you can still make it worth your while.

If you find it hard simply to choose a number and stick with it, another way to set reasonable limits for your shopping budget is to work backward. Take out some of your favorite items from your dresser and closet and take stock of your **price per item value**. Think back to how much your favorite shirt cost. Those perfectly tailored pants? Your pink lambswool cardigan? You can arrive at a number that's worked for you in the past and will likely work in the future. Of course, this can be tough when you found that terrific item at a thrift store, but just remember: if it can happen once, it can happen again.

Jane, a jewelry maker and graduate student in Boston, prefers setting a monthly sum as her limit. She keeps all her after-rent spending to $200. That includes food, drink, clothes, and entertainment. The low number makes her shopping a fun challenge, a DIY adventure. "I know how much I have to spend and I don't spend any more than that," she reasons.

Lisa, a twenty-six-year-old shopper by trade and a writer by profession in Brooklyn, allocates a quarterly sum for her clothing. Every three or four months, she'll head over to the discount department store Century 21 and drop $50 to $60. A pair of shoes, a sweater, a pair of pants, and there it is: insta-wardrobe revitalization. "It keeps my wardrobe updated," she explains.

Jeannie, a former writer for Bluefly.com who now works as an advertising copy writer in Detroit, allocates money paycheck to paycheck, which keeps things neat for her. "I'll set aside a certain amount of each paycheck and use it for clothes."

Summer, an artist in Brooklyn, allows herself to buy a great pair of sneakers when she's had a good month. But when the money is slow, she doesn't like to shop at all.

Personally, I like to take a more wait-and-see approach to shopping. While I always keep an eye on what I spend, I'll rollover my balance, so to speak, if nothing calls to me and I have no immediate need. Some months, when I'm so busy I don't even have time to shop (work can be a blessing in disguise), I reward myself with a treat a few weeks later. That way, I don't have to go overboard with the number crunching, but I can also stay in fiscal shape.

Also, when I know there's a big closeout sale at one of my favorite stores coming up at the end of a season, I'll avoid buying anything for a few months so that I can invest my money in fabulous pieces rather than a fistful of trendy T-shirts from Gap.

Now comes the fun part: scoring the most for the least amount of money. Consider your urban environment one big treasure hunt. Retail prices are predators, sales are manna. Here is your crib sheet, your Style Survival Guide.

STEP TWO: SHOP AROUND

You don't rent an apartment without scoping out listings in the neighborhood. And you certainly don't buy a computer without checking prices around town and various Web sites. So why set out with your sights on one item while turning a blind eye to the competition? If you're in need of a spring skirt in something other than black and you have a few hours to kill, treat a day of comparison shopping like speed dating, that eponymous new method of cramming the most blind dates into the smallest amount of time. Like bad boyfriend pairings, you'll know right away if the item is right. Clothes may not be balding, have bad breath, or gloat about lame jobs, but they have their equivalent sticking points. You'll know immediately if they're strike-outs or scores. Still, it takes skills to flirt with shop owners, play the field, and only give it up when you're good and ready. Try these well-worn phrases, you coy thing you:

"Let me slip into something a little more comfortable."

Heading out for a day of shopping? Forgo the Ferragamos and opt for walk-friendly slides. After ten minutes of mall-prancing, you'll be desperate for a new pair of shoes, even if you don't need them. At the same time, while dressing down, don't make the mistake of looking the shlump. A neatly-put-together ensemble puts you in the right frame of mind to buy the best possible clothes—and get the best service.

Pull your hair back in a neat ponytail and put on a little makeup. If you look like you just rolled out of bed, everything you put on will look like PJs. But if you look ready for a close-up, the clothes you try on will be that much more appealing.

"I'm just looking."

Even if you're looking for something specific, this hedgy phrase will free you from clinging shop owners. Wander on your own terms, peruse as you please, and shake off suggestions about what the shop owner thinks would look f*aaabbul*ous.

Shop owners are always trying to push me into outfits, pairing shirts with cute pants or sweaters with the matching shell. I'm not the outfit type; sweater sets say suburban soccer mom to me. Plus, I find that the brash pairings blur the line between what I might want and what I need. I have to remind myself what my goals are.

I can't tell you the number of times I've watched a girl stand in front of a mirror, tugging a pair of too-tight pants. "Does this make me look fat?" she'll awkwardly the salesgirl. More often than not, I hold myself back from jumping in with a "Don't do it!" Even if the salesgirl says no, pants that make you feel squirmy and squish your tush aren't going to get much wear, no matter how convincing a compliment from a salesperson with an eye on commission may be.

"I need to think about it."

If a piece of clothing makes the cut, but the price is higher than you would like to spend, don't be afraid to speak up. "I need some time to think about it," is a perfectly acceptable thing to say.

If possible, put the contender on hold for as long as the shop will allow; the more time the better. This is your opportunity to survey all your options. Don't get bullied into buying something that doesn't suit you.

To do that, forgo the chaperone and stay single in your endeavors. Elisabeth Filarski, from *Survivor*, who has a show on the Style Network called *The Look For Less*, prefers shopping alone. She recalls wistfully a blue and white coat with polka dot lining she tried on in London with a male friend. He counseled her against buying it. But then, after walking around all day, she couldn't stop thinking about the coat. When she got back to the store, it was closed down for the day—and she was leaving town the next morning. But as fate would have it, she spotted the store owner on the street and begged him to open the store for five minutes to sell her the coat. And he did! The incident made her realize that if you're thinking about something, go get it.

Trust your intuition. And trust your instinct. "Go with your gut," advises Debi Greenberg, the president of Louis Boston, a unique, upscale, longtime family-owned men's and women's store. "If you see it and you like it, you should buy it," she says, "because that is so rare."

My friend Sari still regrets not trusting her gut while shopping at the Prada store in Italy with a friend. She was deciding between two bags, one seasonal and one practical. She immediately fell in love with the seasonal one, but talked herself out if it. "What if it just becomes 'last season's bag?'" she reasoned, and ended up buying the practical one. "Now, every time I wear my bag, all I think about is that I wanted the other bag." If you feel the tug of a piece, instinctually, and you know you want it, go with it.

Alternately, if you're feeling wishy-washy, walk on. Don't waste your money. There are enough clothes in the sea that you need not compromise on almost-there wares.

"I'll call you..."

If you choose to put a possible skirt on hold, leave the shop with a good impression; you don't want them to feel like you're speed shopping or leading them on. As you tear off to take a look at some other skirts, toss off a smile and a "Thanks!" Leave with a promise, and make sure the door remains open for you to come back.

"It's not you, it's the skirt."

If you're certain Store Number 1's skirt doesn't make the cut, don't lead them on by putting the item on hold. It's a waste of their time and it may prevent another Urban Girl from getting her hands on the goods.

Be honest without being hurtful to a boutique owner. Too cheap-looking, ugly, last year; it all may be the case, but keep it to yourself. An Urban Girl knows what she likes—and what she doesn't—but more importantly, she knows when to be demure and gracious, when etiquette trumps the truth.

STEP THREE: CLOTHES INSPECTION 101

You don't buy a car without taking a look under the hood. So why invest in clothes without a similar scientific diagnostic? Take out your specs and read the fine print. Feel the seams. Is the thread loose and sparse? Flip the shirt over. Tug on the fabric. Does it resist evenly? Are there strings hanging off? You don't need a magnifying glass to see a disaster in the works, such as a tear in progress or a misshaping in the making.

Do the fabrics pass the test?
Scratch test
- Pull the garment taut and drag your finger across quickly and solidly.
- It passes if the drag leaves no mark
- It fails if you can see the streak

TIP: reasonable measures

In five years, when you're making more than your age in salary, you may be able to drop $50 on a spanking new T-shirt. But for today, it's budget time. Here are some valuable price guidelines that will help you find what you need.

$20—T-shirts, tank tops, belts
$40—cotton sweaters, blouses, summer pants
$50—pants, dresses, wool sweaters, sneakers
$100—jeans, cashmere sweaters, shoes, wool winter pants
up to $200—coats, bags, fancy shoes

Scrunch test

- Grab a bunch of the fabric in your palm and mush it together for five seconds. Release.
- It passes if there are no lasting wrinkles
- It fails if the garment is rumpled

Scrub test

- Take two pieces of the garment and rub them together vigorously.
- It passes if you can't see the beginnings of nubby pills forming
- It fails if the fabric starts to ball up above the surface

One step in your fabric diagnostic is to conduct a close study of the materials. "If you really want the best fabrics, look at the balance of the weave or knit and the size of the yarn," advises Janice Stone, a professor of Textiles and Clothing at Iowa State University.

GENERAL SHOPPING STRATEGIES
Always keep your eyes on the prize

Urban Girls always follow the cardinal rule of the Russian School of Shopping: snatch up the good stuff when you see it because you never know if you'll be able to find it tomorrow. Luckily, in this country, we've never needed to apply that to staples like toilet paper and toothpaste, but some have taken the rule to new levels.

My friend Jane was perusing the racks at BCBG one afternoon last year. She had just gotten engaged to her boyfriend, and her

TIP: top notch signs:

- Single-needle stitching
- Tight stitching, at least fourteen per inch
- French cuffs
- Cross-stitched buttons
- Durable fibers

eyes were cast wide for any wedding attire ideas. She knew that she didn't want to do the conventional wedding dress thing, but she had no idea exactly what she was looking for. But on this day, Jane hit the jackpot: a sheer white blouse for $100. Jane knew she had to have it, even though the wedding was a year away and there was no matching bottom for the top.

Still, she packed the blouse away in her closet, prayed that it wouldn't be bad luck, and eventually wore it down the aisle a year later with a lovely flowy skirt. *Pas mal.*

Some savvy Urban Girls like to take the rule to the next level, not only buying one perfect item that pops up out of the blue, but doubling or tripling up. Sari learned her lesson after buying the Perfect Pair of Shoes. Comfortable suede slip-ons with just enough heel to give her calves and posture a sexy lift, the shoes seemed destined for every outfit she composed from her closet. But after wearing them day in and day out, the Perfect Pair of Shoes quickly became far from it, as the suede scuffed and the heels flattened.

A year later, Sari frantically tried to order three more pairs from the designer. Needless to say, the shoes had been discontinued, and Sari was out of luck. "I *so* wish that I'd bought three pairs when I originally bought them," she lamented.

If you know immediately when you see an item of clothing that it is going to become well-worn, consider stocking up, especially if the price is right.

Don't be swayed by sales stickers

A 50 percent off markdown on $1,000 is still too much to pay for a pair of leather pants with a droop in the butt. Compelling though the sticker may be, don't overlook obvious duds.

We've all done it before—convinced ourselves that the shoes *sorta* fit, that the sweater really doesn't make us look too busty, that, uh-huh, yellow is a terrific color for our pasty selves. But then you get home, you stash the new goods away, and you never wear them.

Mistakes I've made getting wooed by what looks to be a good deal include:

- Shoes that are a teensy bit too tight. You never wear shoes unless they're comfortable! Even when they're cheap.
- Sweaters with droopy arms. Snug arms are always the sexiest.
- Pants a little too tight around the waist. It feels gross to end the day with lines around your belly. No thanks.
- Clothes to shrink into. You'll only feel bad about yourself looking at what you have that you can't wear. Buy in your current size, not the one you aspire to.

Discount decoding

Fifteen percent, 30 percent, 70 percent off. They're all better than nothing, but after the 50 percent markup that most department stores take, some discounts just bring you back down to heavily overpriced merchandise. So when is enough enough?

A former executive from Macy's in San Francisco offers this piece of advice: "Go for anything 30 percent or higher." Any discount under that figure isn't really a discount. The first week, markdowns start at 25 percent, next week they move to 30 percent, then 40 percent, and then 50 percent is usually the final step.

know your fabrics

	Cotton	Linen	Silk	Wool
Benefits	Durable, absorbent	Absorbent, cool, strong	Strong, cool; repels dirt; doesn't shrink	Doesn't wrinkle or stretch; resilient; hard to muss
Downsides	Shrinks up to a full size; lets out heat when wet; flammability	Wrinkles easily	Wrinkles easily; can be expensive to clean	Can pill and shrink

But no matter the discount, the price can't be right if the fit isn't. To make sure you're not making any rash purchases, take a moment to think about if you'd find that slightly flawed item just as compelling at full price. Wavering? Put it aside.

STEP FOUR: TIMING IS EVERYTHING
Shopping by season

The necessity of the annual September back-to-school shopping spree is engrained in our heads, but it is actually a bad idea, even if there are sales. Whenever possible, buy out of season. Bathing suits in the bitter cold; coats in the humid days of summer; spring hats when all in God's name you want is a fluffy muff. It's counterintuitive to buy items that you can't use right then, but that's precisely why it's a good idea.

When no one else wants something, chances are you can head in for the kill. Prices fluctuate in stores according to supply and demand. And you better believe that demand wanes for linen pants when there's a bed of snow on the ground. Cash in on being off.

In the same way that the day after Thanksgiving is a nightmare for holiday shopping in terms of crowds, the month after Christmas can be a gift for bargain hunters.

Many American stores, like their European counterparts, have blowout sales twice-yearly. For example, upscale hip clothing store Louis Boston, in Boston, has a terrific sale every July and January, in which everything in the store is 50 percent off. The same goes for Barneys in New York and Neiman Marcus nationally.

Small boutiques tend to follow the same seasonal sale schedule— the January/July clean-up. The stores need to make room for next season. Help them out by taking some clothes off their hands! This is one of those times when having cleaned out your closet to make way for the new pays off.

Also keep your eye out for similar end-of-season sales at other stores, where January/February and July/August can bring as much as 80 percent off sales.

Shopping by month

Items at big department stores always go on sale according to a schedule. They all follow set-in-stone calendars for when items will go on sale. And if the stores haven't made their sales projections for a particular month, they'll just start the sale early.

Best of all are preseason sales when you're in the market for a winter coat. Pass the racks of bathing suits in July and August and pick out next season's winter coats, with a healthy 30 percent discount. You can try them on, order one, and pick it up in October. (The coats the department store has in stock preseason are for fitting, so you have to wait a few months to get your new coat. A small price to pay, eh?)

Follow this calendar and time your buying choices wisely:

January: Boots, cocktail dresses, hats, scarves, European designer lines, housewares

February/March: Winter sweaters (further discounts), resort clothes. Outlet stores knock down their prices now too. Big money to be saved!

April: Spring gear, tights and socks, sheets

May: Bathing suits and gear

June: Sunglasses, handbags

July/August: Sheets and bedding; summer gear, including shorts, flip flops, tank tops, short-sleeved shirts, skirts, sandals, winter coats

September: Anything in denim

October: Rain gear; trench coats; women's suits; winter pants; fall clothes

November/December: Leather gloves; cashmere scarves; tablewares

Shopping by day

The three key days for shopping are Tuesday, Thursday, and Friday.

Tuesday

Big department stores find any reason to throw a big sale. *A Heat Wave Broke! 40% off all watches!* Or *Spooky Halloween Sale! 20% off bedding!*

who knew?

Shopping out of climate works just as well. Las Vegas stores may do a brisk business in lamé tanks and hot pants, but you can bet good money that snow boots and wool turtlenecks aren't big sellers. Bathing suits in Alaska, fleece in Texas...you get the idea.

Clip the newspaper ads, but then disregard the dates. While the stores announce that sales start on Thursday or Friday, a little birdie from Macy's tells us that the clothing in question is already tagged as early as Tuesday, right after the execs come out of their Monday meeting where they decide what goes on sale. Get first dibs before the masses descend!

Thursday

Thursday is Sale Day at Gap, Banana Republic, and Old Navy, which are all run by the same company. After an item has been in the store for between eight and twelve weeks, the managers will tag it for the sales rack, depending on how well it's selling at full price. Store employees find out the day before the items go on sale, so make friends with your fellow mall rats and be ready to jump on Thursday morning when you hear from your buddies behind the counter. *Your favorite cropped khakis are now half price!*

Friday

Gigi Guerra, an editor at *Lucky* magazine, says her absolute favorite day to go shopping is Friday. Some weekend sales start Friday evenings, and at the end of a long workweek, it's a nice way to reward yourself. You get first dibs on the goods, the stores are generally empty, and you are primed to do yourself right for all of your hard work.

BEYOND THE SALE: OTHER STRATEGIES FOR IN-STORE SAVINGS
Price adjustment policies: Keep your receipts

Your mom always told you to keep the receipts. But do you?

Befriending salespeople doesn't cost you a thing and it just may pay off. Deal with the same person each time you visit a store. Starting a relationship with your favorite store's employees may compel them to give you the heads-up about an upcoming sale. Remember, a score for you could be a commission for them. Drop off your card next time you sign your credit card receipt.

This is one of those times when Mom knows best.

Think of keeping your receipts as your ticket to free money. Many stores maintain price adjustment policies, giving you cash back if your recent purchase has dropped in price. At some places, the window of opportunity to cash in on subsequent sales is two weeks, other places it's a month, but without your receipt, it's never. Never heard of it? That's no surprise. Often times they tuck the policy away next to the register in really fine print. Hone in, eagle eye.

I recently got into the habit of holding on to my receipts and always keeping my eye on stores' price adjustment policies. My most recent discount victory was with a black shoulder bag from Nine West, which plummeted in price right after I purchased it. I marched right back in with the receipt (I keep them in my wallet for a few weeks) and got cash back. It's money in the bank!

For those who prefer to keep their wallets clean of scraps of paper, there are trusty alternatives. Make it easy on yourself. Put an envelope in a frequented spot in your apartment (your mail stash, your desk, front and center on the kitchen table) and just toss your receipts in when you come home. Next time you're heading out and plan on passing by stores you recently visited, take the envelope with you. That scarf you bought at Banana Republic may just have dropped $30—just enough to cover tonight's impromptu dinner with your long-lost friend from grade school!

Sample sales

Keep an eye on your local magazines and papers. Many designers frequently open up their showrooms for sample sales, slashing prices as much as 60 to 80 percent off, if you're lucky. The sales can be madhouses, but it's worth a visit. Get there early, and wear versatile clothing that you can layer in case there isn't a dressing room. Beware that you'll have to brave the crowds, especially for the famous ones, like the Sigerson Morrison sale in New York, where the $350 shoes are slashed to $99.

Find out about sample sales at:
- *New York* magazine, www.newyorkmetro.com
- *Time Out New York*, www.timeoutny.com
- www.Lazarmedia.com
- www.dailycandy.com
- www.samplesale.com
- www.nysale.com

Thrift scores

There's *nothing* like the thrill of a thrift score.

From my first real score, I was hooked. It was junior year of college and I was shopping with my family friend Penny, who taught me almost everything I know about bargain hunting. We were at the Salvation Army on the Upper West Side and she was riffling through racks while I shuffled my feet, prepared to go. But Penny wasn't quite ready, so I wandered into the back room and absentmindedly flipped through a rack of dress pants. And then I found them, vintage Yves Saint Laurent wool slacks in navy blue for $6. They fit me perfectly. It was fate.

And thus was born the thrift score.

From then on, I began to take thrift store shopping—and the subsequent scores—as a matter of personal worth, pride, panache. Hell, sometimes it doesn't even matter what the thing looks like, as long as I

a sampling of national stores that maintain their own price adjustment policies:

Time limit, with receipt, your window is:

Banana Republic	14 days
Gap	14 days
J. Crew	14 days
Limited	10 days
Old Navy	7 days
Urban Outfitters	14 days
Macy's	10 days

got a *deal*. Oh, this *shmatteh*, I might say, all fake-casually. "Nine bucks!" The value of the score feels almost more delightful than the perfect-fitting pants.

Concetta, a rapper in New York who goes by the name of Princess Superstar, has cultivated a look she proudly describes as "white trash." Scouring the local thrift stores around New York, she's found an amazing selection of diverse garments that suited her small budget when she was getting started in her music career, working two jobs and trying to put out her first album. Thrifting has allowed her to pair old and new, Gucci with vintage, Puma with thrift scores.

But wandering into an overrun shop can be a dizzying, sometimes smelly experience. Here's how to wade through the wares with minimum time spent, gross garments touched, and bad-buy mistakes.

Location, location, location

Thrift stores in big cities can often be picked clean or overpriced. That's why Dagny, 26, prefers doing her thrift store shopping at home in Reno. She's riffled through stores in San Francisco, Boston, New York, and Chicago, but she's never found the variety and the deals in those cities as she has in Reno. Just think about it. Next time you're on a road trip or visiting a friend in a small college town, hit the thrift stores. This is one time when the big city doesn't pay off.

That's certainly something that Elisabeth Filarski knows as well. When she's on location for her show on the Style Network, or when she's traveling with her husband, who plays for the Philadelphia Eagles, she always makes sure to hit the local out-of-town thrift stores. "Any time I'm on a trip, I'll check out vintage stores," she says. "When people are away from

New York and L.A., they let things go that they should hold on to. Those are always the places that have the best stuff. I usually try to find a vintage store wherever I am."

Susan Orlean, a *New Yorker* writer and author of *The Bullfighter Checks Her Makeup*, also recalls being dismayed by the dearth of good thrift store finds when she moved from small-town Portland to big-city Boston and then New York. "It was really tough to find good stuff," she remembers. "There's no question that the Goodwill in Portland has more than the Goodwill in Boston." In a small town, she says, the vintage finds can also be particularly good. "In Portland, there were lots and lots of reasonable vintage stores. They were run by the people who went to the Goodwill and found the nice stuff and increased the price a little, but it was still affordable."

Pick your battles

It's easiest to conquer a store when you have a sense of what you might be looking for. Christie, 23, a student at Fashion Institute of Technology in

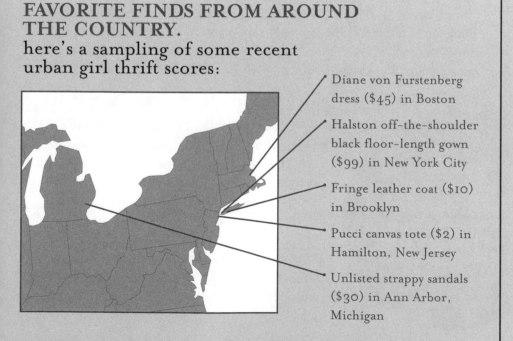

FAVORITE FINDS FROM AROUND THE COUNTRY.
here's a sampling of some recent urban girl thrift scores:

Diane von Furstenberg dress ($45) in Boston

Halston off-the-shoulder black floor-length gown ($99) in New York City

Fringe leather coat ($10) in Brooklyn

Pucci canvas tote ($2) in Hamilton, New Jersey

Unlisted strappy sandals ($30) in Ann Arbor, Michigan

New York, always starts with accessories. Then shoes. Then clothes. It's an approach that helps her feel immediately comfortable riffling through the racks at any store she wanders into.

Set your selection criteria

A rack of hundreds of blue pants in varying shades can be daunting. Where to start? With your hand to the rack, first feel for quality fabrics, then look at the shade, and, only then, try the item on for cut and fit. You'll waste your time if you do it in reverse. A pair of pants that fits well but is itchy and stained all over isn't exactly a Must Buy.

Consignment shopping: thrifting's fancy sister

If your heart is set on Manolo Blahniks, but your budget is more Steve Madden, don't give up hope. Many consignment stores specialize in designer duds. The prices are significantly higher than at thrift stores, but the quality is often much higher as well. A recent trip to a local shop in Boston yielded Diesel jeans ($50 as opposed to $130) and black ankle-high stiletto Manolo Blahniks ($90). Head to the fancy neighborhoods in town to do the best consignment shopping because these are usually the stores where socialites unload last season as soon as the new gowns come in. With thrift store shopping, you want to head to the hills to find the best deals, but with consignment stores you want to hone in on high-income bracket neighborhoods.

Log on

These days, some of the best bargains are found after the letters www. Web sites like Bluefly.com and Mightyflirt.com offer great prices on designer wares. But shopping online is especially tricky with shoes and personalized clothing.

Know your size in various lines

If you are familiar with what size you take in the line you are buying, you reduce the chance that you'll have to shoulder more shipping expenses when returning the ill-fitting items.

Know the true value
Be well aware of the value of the item you're buying. If it's Marc Jacobs shoes you're after, know exactly the model and fit of the shoes you plan on buying. That way, you can know immediately if you're getting a deal or simply getting duped.

Be prepared for shipping costs and more shipping costs
Unless you're hooked up with shipping-free coupons, ordering over a website tacks on added expenses for shipping, which can add up fast!

Leavin' la ladies' department
Yes, yes, you like long walks on the beach, chardonnay, getting your nails done. You're a *girl*. But sometimes it pays to think outside the box. Why feel compelled to always shop in the ladies' department? Break out of the mold; get in touch with your Y chromosome and your inner twelve-year-old.

Oftentimes, boys' departments carry big sizes of similar styles, and little girls' stores carry funky ironic items. The prices are lower, the style is more whimsical, and the benefits are big. Here's where cross-dressing pays:

Shoes
Dagny's favorite pair of shoes for a while was a pair of high-top leather Reeboks for boys. "They're my little boy's basketball shoes," she announced with glee. She found them at a boys' sporting goods store for half price.

Trendy tees
Deb, a thirtysomething editor in New York, has a favorite store, Wet Seal. Yup, that's right. The trendy mall establishment that looks to outfit teen pop idols in all their distressed denim and fringe tanks. Delia's works just the same. Little girls' clothes mean little girls' prices.

Underwear

Über-trendy department store H&M always stocks a wide selection of little boys' boxer-briefs in playful colors and patterns.

Socks

Little girls' uniform stores are a great place to stock up on accessories and ironic outfits. Find treasures like mini-blouses with frill collars, tiny kilts, and socks with yellow ducks quacking around your ankles.

Gap Kids

If you wear a size 4 or under in women's, you can probably squeeze into clothing from Gap Kids. Not only is it much cheaper, but you can also find fun hats and little preppy polos that fit perfectly. Susan Orlean still swears by Gap Kids. "I buy children's clothes when I can because they're so much less expensive and they usually happen to fit me," she says. "Gap Kids fits me better, in many instances, than grown-up Gap. And it's cheaper." Orlean also likes little boys' Hanes undershirts. "They look really nice and they're cheap. Even though I can afford to choose differently now, I still would rather not waste money if I can avoid it."

Ralph Lauren boys' department

Pillage this boys' department for all your preppy needs at lower prices than the adult line. Move beyond the obvious button-down shirts and boys' oxfords—which fit perfectly—to suits, which you can pick up for no more than a few hundred dollars. Girls with hips may find it tricky, but if you're cut like Mick Jagger, narrow, lanky, and slim, the suits are chic and half off what you'd normally pay.

chapter sixteen

style staples

"The great thing about vintage is that it's neither in fashion nor out of fashion, so it doesn't come or go."

—Susan Orlean, author of
The Bullfighter Checks Her Makeup

it would be nice to be able to have your couture and wear it too. Perusing the racks at the sample sales, the thrift stores, and the consignment shops, you may want *everything*. Unfortunately, unless your name is Nicky or Paris, the bottom line in your checkbook dictates No Can Do. The Urban Girl must set priorities. In our current mode of living, the lifestyle of the not-at-all-rich and not-yet-famous, we must be realistic. Like her kitchen pantry, the Urban Girl's well-endowed, well-maintained closet will pay off in the end, saving her money.

There's no need to sit down at your PC with a spreadsheet, price per wear figures, and pro and con lists. Clothing tends to fall into categories. There are certain things you will need to replenish on a regular schedule and others that are a one-time, one-shot deal.

If you can keep your wardrobe in slight rotation, it won't tire as quickly and will hold up longer. That's why I'm always in the market for undershirts, underwear, and good socks. Having pretty undergarments makes me feel like I'm treating myself well. During the holidays a few years ago, a friend's grandmother gave me a gift of some long, extraordinarily soft Ralph Lauren cotton socks. At the time, I thanked her graciously, thinking it was perhaps an unusual item to give someone. But the socks immediately became a wonderful fixture in my wardrobe, the first pair I selected after doing the laundry. The soft calf-hugging firm socks left me feeling pampered.

LOOK FOR MULTI-USE RATHER THAN STAND-ALONE ITEMS

Once you've set down your monthly clothing allowance, figure out what your priorities are. You're not going to blow it all on a white T-shirt, however snug the spandex and crisp the seams. You're also not going to divvy up the number fair square, even steven on Every. Single. Item. Of. Clothes. *Yawn*. Geez, we're talking shopping here, not clinical research.

Certain parts of your clothing repertoire deserve a larger proportion of the loot. Things you'll wear more than once; things you won't kick yourself for removing the price tag from; things that end up practically paying *you*.

Frequent buys	Rare occasion
Belts	Cocktail dress
Shoes	Raincoat
Socks	Red anything (keep your zingers to lipstick)
Underwear	Impossibly high heels
Bras	
Tights	

Every item in my closet must do double-duty; every shirt, every pair of pants, every *shoe* is a two-timing affair. "I would never buy anything that only went with one thing," advises Kelly, a thirty-four-year-old personal shopper and boutique owner in Boston.

When picking out a new piece, take a moment to picture what it will go with. If you're struggling, think twice, because you may be setting yourself up for a pricier purchase in the long run when you have to buy *more* clothes to work with this new piece.

I was recently shopping with my friend Emily, a twenty-five-year-old executive. Wandering in and out of stores, we came across a pair of red-and-white striped low heels. They were truly knockouts. She held them up, oohing and sighing. They only had a size 8 (Emily's). All signs pointed to "Buy Me!" But the price tag ($220) wasn't going to be the only splurge. Buying the shoes meant that Emily was going to have to buy a new suit to go with the shoes, a proposition that would have put her out an additional $300 to $400. And the shoes would then be paired with only one outfit. All told, in the end, the seductive heels lost their allure. No multitasking, no deal.

TIP: key ideas

- Selecting all items in fabrics that will work well together will make your wardrobe work best for you.
- When in doubt, buy in black. It masks flaws in less expensive fabrics and generally looks good whether you bought it at Marshalls or Neiman Marcus.
- Avoid bells and hoops and opt for clean lines. A piece of clothing will be more versatile in the end.

Suits

The ideal suit will be composed of three parts: a fitted jacket with lovely lapels; a slim skirt without too much of a butt-hug; and straight-lined pants. It will be composed of a thin wool, rather than crepe or rayon, which is only good for one season. The jacket can be paired with jeans, pants, or any other skirt, as long as the colors work well together. If you're working in blacks, simply shine a bright light on the two fabrics or inspect under natural light to make sure the colors don't clash. And the skirt and pants immediately become stand-out elements in a wardrobe.

TIP: itemize what's important

Think of your clothing as falling on a continuum. On a scale of Always need to replenish ($) to Better to buy once every few months ($$) to Clothes you need almost never ($$$):

$
socks
underwear
bras
exercise clothes
basic white and black T-shirts
belts
button down shirts

$$
sweaters
sneakers
flats
jeans
suits
dress pants

$$$
dresses/skirts
iconic couture items

Slingbacks

The perfect pair of shoes—comfortable yet cool—is tough to find. A great, thin black sling-back may be just the ideal item. You can throw on the shoes with jeans to add *élan* to an outfit or you can wear with a suit to dress it up. Every time I buy a pair of shoes I think about whether it would work with skirts *and* pants.

Dress

Molly, twenty-six, a radio producer, has one black leotard dress. She normally wears it to yoga. But when she had to head to a ritzy suburban bridal shower, the garb Molly generally used for downward-facing dogs made the transition to upward-facing white wine toasts. A good stretchy fabric, combined with cute shoes and dangly elegant earrings helped the dress make the switch from the sticky mat to the white damask couch.

PIECEMEAL SHOPPING

Since buying up a department store isn't an option, you're aiming to get the most bang for your buck. While you may be more accustomed to snatching up small pieces week by week (another T-shirt, cute belt), it's time to change your shopping strategy. Think big. Think of yourself as Investing In Pieces.

Remember those September school clothes shopping trips with Mom where you'd pick up everything you needed for the next six months? Whatever the sales markdown, they're a bad idea, financially and fashionably. Why blow your wad all at once? Come bleak snowy March, your "new" clothes will be blech. And you'll be out of luck...and money.

Buy what you need when you need it. Forgo the blitzkrieg consumeristic extravagance. Fun and opulent as it may be, the rush fades fast. You'll be better off with a piece-by-piece shopping trickle than an annual flood.

But in your new mode of buying fewer numbers of pieces at higher prices, you must forgo the smaller, flittier clothing items. Think of your new mode as ditching quantity for quality. You may have fewer options overall, but you will have more versatility with each piece. Opt for the $100 item rather than the five $20 throwaways.

"Instead of buying the safe things, the same things every time, buy elements," instructs Louis Boston's president and buyer Debi Greenberg. "When you have a blouse from Dries van Noten, use that same blouse with shorts and flip flops in the summer."

SPLURGE WHEN IT STRIKES!

Life would be bananas if a girl didn't go crazy every once in a while. Saddle yourself into buying only slingbacks, and you'll immediately pine for pumps. Decide that denim is a must and corduroy starts looking mighty fine. Like a curfew, rules make you crave bending, extending, and breaking.

Deny yourself a scoop of ice cream on a hot day in summer, and you'll find yourself head-first diving into three later that evening. Create set rules about chocolate, cookies, and cake, and you'll only break them or feel horribly deprived. Sit down to write a complete novel, and you'll stare down a blank page, your eyes blurring at the relentlessly blinking cursor.

Occasional excess is an important part of mindful thrift. It's the yin to the yang. The tonic to your gin.

But being impulsive and indulging I-want-it-now whims can even benefit from savvy shopping smarts. If you're in bad need of retail therapy (and even the most stable girl gets a jones for it occasionally), go for it.

Simply shop with *savoir faire*. Like learning a new language, you memorize the verb charts, dream about subjunctive, passive, informal, and then you toss it all out and head for the hills. Immerse yourself in the language—forget the rules and have fun! Once you know what the rules are, now you can play. Indulge, bend, and break 'em!

TRENDS: LOVE 'EM OR LEAVE 'EM?

As a girl about town, it's hard to turn away from the tug of trends, to deny the allure of this season's distressed denim fetish, of next season's punk rock studded belts, of all-white suits. But on a budget, buying into every season's latest rage is not really an option. So what to do?

Let's face it, ignoring them is impossible. Back when I was working part-time at the *New York Observer* during college, I was first introduced to the coveting instinct to a degree I'd never before experienced. *I see it; I like it; I want it*, went my daily inner dialogue.

Once in the door of the office, which was in an Upper East Side townhouse, I'd peer up from manuscripts and dwell on

who knew?

Feeling like you've got a credit card trigger finger? You're not alone. Forty-six percent of all women admit to making impulsive purchases at the cashier. Don't worry, though. Simply steer your impulsivity towards pieces that will pay off, that you'll keep around for years rather than months.

hemlines, dramatic cuffs, and color pairings. Those days, I focused much of my coveting attention around one particular item: a Kate Spade bag. I distinctly remember the first time I saw the bag. A coworker named Kate casually slung over her shoulder a boxy bag made of a fabric that seemed at once silky and sturdy. The straps were durable, and the black tote carried everything. Yet, there was a daintiness about it, a femininity. The year was 1997, and it was my first encounter with Kate Spade, the eponymous designer who has since shaken up the American handbag, accessories, and cosmetics world.

It was love at first glance. After work, I walked down Madison Avenue on my way to the subway to head cross-town. And before heading back up to campus, I ducked in to Barneys—just to see. I found the display in a corner of the first floor. There were bags of various colors, sizes, shapes. Each one was more sleek, more chic, more, *err*, expensive. The smallest bag, a slim shoulder affair, which would have fit a little lipstick, a cell phone, and a billfold, boasted a price tag solidly north of $100.

I did some mental arithmetic, started some internal negotiation, busted out some rationale about how I could just scrimp and save, deny and delegate funds from elsewhere.

After a few minutes of mental calculations, I wrenched myself away from the bags and decided to sleep on it. One night turned into a few weeks. And while I waited, deciding if it was a purchase plunge I wanted to take, I noticed the bags sprouting up on every undergrad around town. Every girl I saw, it seemed, all of a sudden was flaunting the bag. It was a slap in the face; the boxy bag was everywhere. And so, therefore, it could no longer be cool.

The transition was swift: the fashion pendulum had swung and I still had my $300 in my pocket, and without looking like yesterday's news.

What had happened?

Like neighborhood real estate prices, fashion trends follow a certain pattern. There's a path, players, and ever-shifting boundaries. Keeping abreast of the Next Big Thing is both dizzying and irresistible. It's also expensive.

In real estate, people are always looking for the new hip neighborhood. It's often edgy to begin with, situated in a marginal section of town, such as New York's Williamsburg, San Francisco's South of Market, or Boston's Somerville. Artists congregate in low-price areas; their infectiously creative chic energy rubs off on the hordes, who surge to snatch up recently renovated condos, trying to get in on the vibe, be in the know, buy their way into hip. And then, *pfffft*—the neighborhood becomes too expensive for the unassuming trendsetters. Cool moves a few miles farther east, farther up, farther out. Cool is always an arm's length away.

The same thing goes for style trends. Every season we're introduced to new hemlines, hair colors, and fabrics. I was at Vidal Sassoon in Boston recently, learning about "this season's look." I was told "it's all about" chunky, asymmetrical, irreverent yet somehow feminine. A picture of a model was put in front of me; on her left side, her hair went down to her shoulder and was a deep, stark shade of black. On her right side, she had jagged severe blond Vs. "Like designers, we create looks for the season," I was told by Vidal Sassoon long-time London stylist Tim Hartley. Hair trends?

Crack open the magazines and it's impossible to avoid being bumrushed by news of trends in magazines all the time. Pale is the new skin tone! Strappy sandals are the new footwear! Totes are the new handbag! Curly is the new hairstyle! White is the new black! (Buy me!)

Trend forecasters

How do trends happen? Who decides what will be cool? Oddly enough, it's more a science than an art, more a concerted business decision than a hunch. Remember Pet Rocks? A salesman decided in the 1970s that simply packaging a rock and calling it a pet would appeal to buyers. And it did. Pet Rocks became an instant hit when they were introduced in 1976; within six months, they had sold 1.5 million of the large pebbles.

Similarly, designers employ trend scouts and forecasters to hunt down what you will be coveting next year. These "experts" reportedly charge big retailers and designers as much as six

TIP: famous trend mavens

Chloe Sevigny
Winona Ryder
Kelly Osbourne
Lauryn Hill
Sarah Jessica Parker
Jackie O.

figures to dictate your yearnings. They look at the streets, sift through racks at select boutiques, dig through bins at thrift stores, and peer across the pond to see what Londoners and Parisians are wearing. And then they present it for our consumption. And we do. We eat it up.

Traci, a twenty-three-year-old New Yorker, is a former trend scout for the firm Limited Inc. She was part of a team that would hunt down looks to present to the store's executives. If the look passed muster, it was turned into next season's fashion to hit the rack. "I watch people on the street," she explains. "Younger people, younger kids. They always seem to know what's up."

But also, Traci keeps her eye on Japan, home of out-there, busy color schemes, slavish devotion to labels, and cartoonish fashion excess. "Japan is so futuristic. I guarantee you that anything they're wearing now people we will be wearing in two years."

Looking to the street is the best way to be your own trend maven. All clothing buyers pride themselves on their sidewalk hawk-eye, their ability to turn an afternoon walk into a brainstorming session. How easy to follow suit! Next time you're out running errands, focus on the folks around you. Make eyelet contact.

Following trends: The heroin of chic

The problem is, following trends can seem like a never-ending pursuit and can become a pricey habit—indeed, an addictive one. *Still carrying last season's Gucci bag? For shame! Everyone's on to Marc Jacobs, didn't you know?*

When something becomes *en vogue*, chances are the price rises exponentially, immaterial to the quality of the piece. And then it's on to the next $300 handbag. The next $400 shoes. The next $50 cut of khakis.

As former *Harper's Bazaar* editor and *Vogue* alumna Kate Betts noted in the *New York Times*, a trend can cause price hikes faster than you can say Katayone Adeli. Writing about a boutique specializing in skate gear, she marveled that "Twenty-year-old sneakers that had originally

who knew?

A&E television recently selected their top ten fads of the millennium. The one fashion item they chose was the miniskirt. Short and sweet.

who knew?

cost around $45 were going for $300, and $10 T-shirts were fetching $190."

Designers themselves marvel at the astounding markups. While participating as a guest on Elisabeth Filarski's *The Look for Less*, on the Style Network, Cynthia Rowley took Elisabeth on a hunt for a new low-cost outfit through the tag sales of Westchester county. Holding up a white prairie skirt, she smiled, "This is, like, a dollar or something, and by next season it'll be in my stores for $150."

How fast do tomorrow's trends turn into yesterday's old duds? That's the million dollar question. James Twitchell, a pop consumerism expert and author of *Living it Up: Our Love Affair with Luxury*, says it's almost immediate. "I don't have to do any research to tell you that trends turn in a matter of hours. It's very fleeting; it's very shiny; and it lasts just a very short amount of time."

But banishing trends altogether seems ultimately unrealistic. It's just not going to happen. The fact remains, we're girls. We want things; we can't help it. We pine over preppy chic J. Crew T-shirts, we fancy Coach handbags, and we covet Louis Vuitton's hair clasps. Sure, they're impractical, extravagant, absolutely excessive, utterly of the moment. But they also tug at our purse strings—and our hearts.

The key is not denying the allure of trends; it's choosing the right ones. Done right, the clothes will wear out faster than the look. We read, look, and listen. With an eye on the street, we try to get it right.

Sure, it may be love at first sight, but will it be a one-night stand or a long-term relationship?

Sleep on it

See a fabulous shirt in the pages of *W*? Waiting until tomorrow is often a good idea. If the item haunts you and gets incorporated into a fashion fantasy, then chances are—however fleeting—it may be worth it for you. But if the impulse strikes once and not again, *fuggedaboutit*.

Think before you click

Ah, the World Wide Web. Haven of multitasking. We type away, surf the latest looks on Style.com, and chit-chat on message boards as we field calls from friends (um, I mean, *clients*). But what we don't want to do is impulsively press "Purchase" at discount Web sites. Clunky flat camper shoes (in orange!) at 50 percent off are still something you would not have bought otherwise.

Look into it

Perusing Bill Cunningham's *New York Times Sunday Styles* spread and heading out immediately to pick up a wide-brim hat, riding gear, a saddle bag, and a white coat is too easy. Refrain from following trends and start forming them yourself. That way you can *make* the pages rather than read them.

Check the tree rings for time

Is the trendy item in middle age or merely budding? Two years ago, Traci set her sights on the one-shoulder, Amazonian shirt. The look certainly wasn't new. When I was studying abroad in Italy in 1997, my friend Emily picked one up in mauve at a trendy European shop in Florence. At that time, they were all over the place. So three years later, the one-shoulder look was in New York. How long could it last? By the time she'd bought in, it was already almost over. "I bought one," Traci recalls, "and I thought it was the *coolest* thing. But then it went cheeseball so fast." Since she bought retail, her loss was significant. Traci doesn't regret getting in on the one-shoulder garb, she just wishes she did it cheaper. "It would have been safer to go the vintage route instead of full-price," she says ruefully.

Is it of the moment, hour, or year?

Does it say 2003, or this decade? Jane has a rule of thumb. Slim, sleek, and savvy, Jane always has an eye on what's hip. She devours fashion magazines monthly, and checks in on message boards where people discuss the latest look in denim, what Julia Roberts was wearing on the last red carpet she glided down, and Jennifer Aniston's hair products. But she has one rule of thumb when picking out her clothes: "If it's something that someone is going to look at me next season and say, 'Oh, that's *soooo* Winter 2002,' then I definitely won't buy it."

Short attention span style: Fast faders in recent years

Graffiti: Sprouse threw his tag on Louis Vuitton bags, women lined up on wait lists to get theirs (up to $1,000), and within a year, Target pool floaties bore the same stylish graffiti imprints. Graffiti crossed the train tracks and lost cred—quick style, yo.

Cowboy hats: Once the province of herding beef-cakes in the Wild Wild West, cowboy hats started to grace the heads of ironic East Village hipsters as early as the late 1990s. But when style maven Madonna took this Southern Rodeo look mainstream, it was *ta-taa* for the headwear.

White: While there will always be a community of those who summer in Nantucket and opt for the all-white look—from couches to walls to pants—the crisp non-color flits on and off of the national radar on an annual basis. The real question is: how long can anything that is immediately sullied upon contact really last?

Shoulder shrugs: These odd garments, made up of long arms connected

who knew?

Remember Elle Woods in *Legally Blonde*? A fashion footwear misstep actually helped her solve a legal case. After interrogating someone on the stand who had been presenting himself as hetero, Elle discovered that he outed himself as gay by dissing her Prada shoes as *so last year*. Thus, she was able to prove that he wasn't having an affair with her client. I rest my case, your honor. Following seasonal trends may be your downfall.

by a flap of knit fabric in the back, but no body, were over before they even began. Does anyone actually wear these?

Razor scooters: As the digiteratis whipped themselves into a Dockers-clad, Teva-wearing, frenzy of Go Team! enthusiasm, this peculiar kid's mode of transportation hit the streets. Adults dropped their skateboards, their bikes, and their walking shoes to ride on this trend train. But before you could say "Hasta la vista, Venture Capital," the scooters were relegated back where they belonged, in suburban garages and curb trash heaps. As adults, we walk, thank you very much.

Fedoras—Already dated. Don't press repeat. Enough said.

Looks that have lasted or have made a comeback

Hush Puppies: Save for falling off the map between the mid-'70s to the mid-'90s, these comfortably clunky colorful shoes exploded after East Village hipsters rediscovered them about ten years ago; the company expanded from selling around thirty thousand in 1994 to about two million just two years later. *Wow!*

Preppy: Lisa Birnbach's brilliantly satirical *Official Preppy Handbook* took a jab at pearls, polo shirts, and pedigree when it came out in 1980. But the tide has turned from satirical to serious in recent years as the crisp manicured Connecticut look has made a comeback with the likes of Lilly Pulitzer, the always chic lines of Ralph Lauren, and the appearance of striped cotton polos everywhere from TJ Maxx to Target.

Trench coats: From Sophia Loren to Lauren Bacall, film noir and sketchy flashers on the subway, the look of a flouncy khaki coat, dropping just to the knee, cinched at the waist, has ever-enduring appeal. The look also easily transfers to dresses and colors beyond khaki.

Black: Those "in the know" will tell us quite certainly that there's a new black. It's pink, they'll announce, definitively. No, no, now it's gray. That's right, gray is now the new black. Do yourself a favor and tune out the dizzying instructions on ever-changing hip hues. Black will *always* be the new black. It's slimming, it goes with everything, and it is the ultimate in urban chic. *Oh, black, we love you so*—nothing can ever replace you.

From trend to timeless

So what makes one look last and another a mere blip on the trend timeline?

Versatility

Fringe denim is hard to pair—and easily pegged to one season. While denim will always be a winner, veer far away from odd cuts that quickly fade. You'll date yourself in denim that's butt-crack or belly-button baring or relentlessly distressed with factory-manufactured holes. Who do you think you are? Christina Aguilera?

Timelessness

There are certain cuts that will always last, no matter the fabric, trendy label, or of-the-moment look. A-line or pencil in skirts, flats in shoes, snug V-necks in sweaters, three-quarter length arms in shirts, boat-necks, straight-legged pants, cardigans, collared shirts. If money is at a premium, invest in items that were chic fifty years ago, thirty years ago, and today. Rose Kennedy religiously wore Lilly Pulitzer in the 1960s, and so do Uptown ladies today. Why? The preppy patterns are timeless.

Reasonable price-points

Last year, turquoise was the big hit. Big chunky necklaces, dramatic earrings, and clunky bracelets were all the rage. Karen Fabbri, the owner of a boutique called Moxie in Boston's Beacon Hill, wanted to buy herself some turquoise accessories, but since it had already been around for a season, she didn't want to go all out just as the trend was possibly waning. "So I bought a pair of simple turquoise dangle earrings and a delicate turquoise bracelet," she explains. "It has the color but I can wear it forever. It won't be pinned on That Year that Turquoise Hit the Floor."

A lower cost, demure bracelet in the color of the moment is more likely to stay in style longer than bulky opulent pieces because it can fly under the radar more easily. If you are a person who likes to follow trends, try buying on the fringes of the latest look. Instead of springing for a pair of $150 designer jeans, buy smaller: lingerie, a wristwatch, cashmere socks. Choose your battles wisely.

Low-frills, low-flash

A Hush Puppy stands the test of time because it is the pinnacle of practicality. Simple lines, comfortable materials, no-fuss frills. Alternately, a cowboy hat is worn in the city specifically to get attention. A long-lasting trend exists more than one season because it doesn't call attention to itself, but is coyly seductive.

Superstore savings on flitty fashion trends

Big-box budget stores are the best place to buy in on ten-minute trends. The prices are low, the lifespan is short, and you can get in on the action without getting above your head. Think more Savvy Sears than Frugal Fanny. What to buy where:

Target: trendy accessories, Britney-inspired halters, crazy-colored housewares, and robes

Wal-Mart: little boys' T-shirts and little girls' lines, like Mary-Kate and Ashley Olsen's new duds

Kmart: the latest side-striped spandex gear for your downward-facing dogs

Get in on the latest trends without breaking the bank

Don't become a casualty of the consumeristic frenzy. Be chic but be smart. Get in on the action without going cash-poor.

How? Follow these trend-savvy steps to choose your trends wisely.

Go small

Last year, just as PBS's gripping faux-reality TV show *Frontier House* was the talk of the country, all of a sudden, prairie life was everywhere. There were prairie skirts, lace-up bustiers, fringe as far as the eye could see. Jeannie opted for one item, rather than the head-to-toe ensemble, by buying one fringe belt. It was just enough to feel like she had

who knew?

About two-thirds of all women pick up their trendy garb at end-of-season sales. Smart girls!

indulged, but not enough to make her feel like she'd played the part of style sucker.

Go outside the box

Sari, a twenty-six-year-old writer in New York, developed a soft spot in her heart for Kate Spade's handbags during college. She opted to buy into the trend, but she took an alternate, less traveled path. Sari bought a messenger-style Kate Spade bag that she was able to use for years. While the small handbags had a short lifespan on the trend radar, buying the same brand but a different cut or model is a good way to avoid dating yourself before you get good use out of your new purchase.

Go neutral

The minute I saw The Coat, I knew it had to come home with me. I was in San Francisco for Thanksgiving, visiting my family, and my sister and I had wandered into Gap in the Castro neighborhood. There was a purple wool coat with lime green lining, marked down to $60. I snatched it up and counted the days until I headed back to the snowy, blistering winter. I'd seen some marvelous feminine colors for coats in the fashion magazines, and here was my chance to buy in. At least that was the idea. Of course, I should have remembered that wise one-liner by Groucho Marx: "I would never want to be a member of a club that would have me as a member." That club was that of the Purple Coat.

Warning Label: the peril of my purple coat quickly became obvious. Gap is every woman's secret. No sooner had I bought my purple coat and started collecting compliments than other little blonde girls with purple coats started popping up—right next to me on subway platforms, walking toward me on the street. In a purple coat, there's no hiding. You're wearing the same coat—and soon blushing the same hue of pink. I'd walk briskly past the similarly dressed women, we'd avoid eye contact, and I'd shake off the embarrassment just in time to see another woman. The coat really was everywhere.

The same thing happened with polka dots. I'd recently bought a black and white knee-length polka dot skirt at Club Monaco on a weekend visit to New York. A few weeks later, I was out to dinner with some authors in town for a reading in Washington, D.C., and one of the authors was wearing the same polka dot skirt, which I then saw her wear on David Letterman a few months later. "I have that same skirt," I offered. "Well, it's a good thing you're not wearing it right now," she responded. How true. In polka dots and purple, there's no avoiding it: you're marked by your recent purchases. And dated by other people buying the same item. At least give yourself some legroom by buying in at a low price.

chapter seventeen

satisfy without spending

"When I was writing for a small newspaper in Lynn, Massachusetts, I didn't have any money! So my girlfriends and I would share clothes. On Friday nights, we'd call dibs on who got what."

—Jill Davis, author of *Girls' Poker Night* and former writer for *The Late Show with David Letterman* i f you make a habit of heading to the ATM and taking out a fistful of dollars before hitting your favorite boutiques, what do you think is going to happen? Of course, the crisp bills will burn a hole in your wallet. You will wander between the racks, spot a particularly sprightly T-shirt, and think to yourself, "Yes, yes. Hmm. $45? Well, I have that right here." And you might just spring for the overpriced cotton T-shirt, the borderline blouse, the too-tight pants, the denim patchwork skirt that will fade from occupying a special place in your heart within weeks. Not a good idea.

Similarly, too many high-balance special offer credit cards may just induce an ill-advised spending spree. It seems like every day the mailman delivers a stack of offers: I'm one of the chosen people. Woo-hoo! A select, gold, platinum, whatever card could be mine! Sure, I look at the balance and think about how many shoes and bags all of those zeros could materialize into. And then I stop for a minute, wake from my consumeristic fantasy, and toss the offers in the trash. No thanks; one credit card has always been enough for me.

SNIP YOUR CARDS

About a year ago, Jane found herself facing an increasingly heavy mountain of debt. She wasn't super extravagant, but still, things were simply adding up. And when in doubt, Jane would just plunk down the plastic card. I visited Jane, a talented jewelry maker, at her home to talk with her for a story I was writing on young artists on the cusp. One of the artists had regaled me with a story of supporting a photography habit by being on welfare; another spoke of simply pinching every penny; but Jane's woe was of another sort. Laying on her worktable, ominously, was a credit card bill, itemizing everything that she couldn't pay back. *DEBT! it reminded her. You owe me big.*

Jane decided the time had come for a change. Painful though it was, she cut up her credit cards, canceling the numbers, and opted for cash. These days, when Jane buys something, anything, from groceries to Marc Jacobs stiletto ankle boots, she pays in cash. Always. For Jane, ditching the cards and going cash-poor every time she buys something has been a great way of weeding through decisions. She can't buy something unless she really, truly has the money, and that's the breaks. Jane still shops all the time, but minus the plastic, she purchases much less, and does so much more wisely.

DEBIT V. CREDIT

I don't think I could do anything as severe as dumping my credit cards. How would I pay for car rentals or airplane tickets over the Internet? But whenever possible, I pay with my debit card rather than credit. That way I can keep an eye on my balance and won't be shocked at the end of the month.

Facing down a list of purchases I forgot I even made, the monthly credit card bill can be a haunting reeducation on how to add. *How could those few things come to that much?* Using my debit card ensures that every time I take out cash, I know exactly how much I really do have in my bank account, rather than having to perform some feat of mental mathematic gymnastics, subtracting what I remember at that moment having bought. The truth is, it's **always** more than you remember. So make it easy on yourself by not charging too much.

WALLETLESS SHOPPING

If your mall adventure is really the research mission you claim it to be, then ditch the wallet alltogether for the mental notes. As you leave for the mall or the boutique neighborhood, leave your wallet behind. Grab an ID, $20 in case of emergency, bus fare, and hit the streets. If you see something you absolutely must have, you can always go back. Put it on hold. But putting in that extra step will ensure that you'll only buy the items that you need or really, really want. The pink Lacoste thin-gauge sweater—marked down 50 percent—may seem like a must-buy if your credit card is burning a hole in your pocket. *Why not?* It whispers seductively in your ear.

But the fact of the matter is that the sweater is just a wee bit too big, and once you remove yourself from the equation, the allure fades fast. Heading back forces you to ask the question, "Do I really want this?"

NOW WHAT?

All of that shopping "research" does you good only if you apply it. When you come home, use those mental notes, that inspiration, and go shopping in your own closet. Christie, twenty-two, a student at the Fashion Institute of Technology, makes a habit of shopping in her own closet—and revising—every few months. She'll use whatever she sees to retool what she already has.

It's a great habit to get into, both to make room for the new and to give your old wares a new lifespan.

Turn it into a one-woman adventure

Throw on a pair of heels, put your hair up, and put on your favorite lady chanteuses. Leona Naess or Mary J. Blige; whatever gets your booty on the dance floor shakin' without shame. Think of it as juice for your upcoming endeavor. Loosen up.

Identify the culprits

Take out the clothes that need the most TLC, whether they're bland and boring or weathered and tired. Decide what your plan of attack will be: new buttons? Crazy stitching? Dramatic shortening?

Revise

Bust out the needle and thread and buttons. Sew away. Once your wares are spruced up, try tossing together unlikely items. You may just hit on some pairing you never would have imagined.

Pair up with Friends
Make friends, cash in on clothes

Some girls find any excuse for a party. Including cleaning out the closet. Lisa, twenty-six, a writer in New York, gets together with a group of friends every few months at one of their apartments, with duffle bags filled with all of the clothes they can't stand anymore. They dump them in a pile in the middle of the room, strip down to their skivvies, and dive in. It's like a department store, minus the clothing costs. The old clothes that have simply been taking up precious space in your tiny closet may just be the free shopping spree your friend has been looking for.

Ground rules for your clothing swap party:

Pair up with like-sized friends: Someone's bound to feel hurt if she's an 8 and everyone else is a 2. Think ahead when you decide who you'll invite so that everyone will be able to fit into the clothes. Remember, even if you're not the same size, shirts are always a good bet. Also, accessories work well for friends of any size.

Don't forget the party favors: It's not a party unless there is food and drink. Price-conscious partiers can opt for the standard pizza and beer combo, but you could also have a potluck or make it simply another occasion for cocktails. And really, what isn't?

Set price limits: Avoid being cheap or unnecessarily fancy. Find out ahead of time what original prices their castaways were. You don't want to show up with arms filled with Banana Republic if everyone else is unloading their Barneys. Get on the same page.

In case of long-term loans, keep insurance: A soiled sweater can ruin a friendship, especially if it's a favorite item. When my formerly favorite Warehouse gray zip-up hooded sweater was returned to me with a bullseye cigarette burn (casualty of a drunken party "oopsie"), I kept my collateral: my trading partner's thinner gray zip-up. My burnt sweater went to the Goodwill; hers is still in my closet. Woo-hoo!

Consider it retail therapy combined with girl time. Do whatever it takes to make a night of it. Braid each other's hair, rent the latest cheesy teen flick, bury yourself in funny articles chronicling the latest Hollywood scandal. Unwind.

Put to use your kindergarten lessons. Share!

Just like Jill Davis, when strapped for cash on a low salary, participate in pseudo-clothing shopping: share the wealth. Pass around your fancy clothes like you do winning sex tips. *I call dibs on the black mini on Friday!*

Don't be afraid to cozy up to your friends' closets. If you're desperate for a one-time only interview suit, borrow instead of buy, and don't hesitate when the girlfriends come a-knockin'. What goes around comes around.

When in doubt, dare to go DIY
Just because something is stale doesn't mean you can't breathe some life into it.

Iron-ons
Spice up your old T-shirts quickly and easily by styling your wares using iron-ons.

- Find a cool image on the web. It can be anything from boxy lettering to retro graphics.
- Buy some iron-on paper. It's sold at office supply stores for around $1 a sheet.
- Print the image out on your iron-on paper.
- Grab an iron and with a few swipes...hello, new shirt.

You can also try it on bags, pants, or whatever you like.

Monogramming
Laverne & Shirley are back. Remember those big swooping L's sewn onto the top of a cardigan? How kitschy but also how *cute*. Simply pull out your mini sewing kit and save yourself a dime.

Alphabet necklaces
Brad Pitt wore one announcing the name of his honey, so did the *Sex and the City* girls. The best bet is that your local craft store stocks the mini cube letters, which you can thread onto some dental floss or a piece of string. It's second grade arts and crafts all over again!

Horseshoe jewelry
When Sarah Jessica Parker sported a horseshoe necklace, the herds headed out to pick up one of the Mia & Lizzie baubles at Fred Segal or

Neiman Marcus, for anywhere from $375 to more than $2,000. But it was easy enough for Jane to make her own. And when the items faded from fashionista favor, Jane was simply out merely the cost of supplies rather than the hefty alternative.

Befriend your tailor

Every Urban Girl needs a tailor she can trust. If hemlines change, she can simply take in her pants to be shortened. If a pair fits well in the butt but is too long, it's certainly worth salvaging. If she finds a great pair of pants on sale that are bulging in odd places, she can still buy them and have

revise a simple T-shirt

- Standing in front of a mirror, tug the fabric tight over your body. Mark off a line where the extra fabric starts. Use scissors to snip off the extra, and sew the two parts together. The best thing about cotton is that it stretches, so if you make your shirt a little small, you can always tug it out.
- Cut the sleeves off so that they turn into cap sleeves, and roll up nicely. And depending on how you like your necklines, snip it low to give cleavage shots or go higher for a demure look.
- Once you've fashioned the shirt to the right shape, grab some accents: curtain bits, old pieces of Chinese patterned dresses, even some chrome foil, and sew them around the neckline. All told, by the end of the day, you've just saved yourself at least a hundred dollars.

here's how to make your own simple T

- Chose your fabric, either a lightweight single or double knit. Pre-shrink the cloth to make sure you don't end up with a baby-T when you're looking for a loose fit.
- Select a pattern in a sewing book that is "for stretch knits only."
- Cut the cloth according to the pattern you chose. Use the smallest seams possible on your first shirt—they're the easiest. Trimming to ¼ or ⅜ inch at neckline, sleeves, and arm holes is best.
- Sew up seams, zigzagging.
- Trim up fabric close to the seam to get rid of excess fabric.
- For neckline and hem, turn under ½ inch and top-stitch.

them fitted to perfection. The trusty tailor is truly a girl's best friend. Do your research and find the perfect one for you.

SHOPPING AS RESEARCH

Growing up, I always preferred reading in a sunroom to wandering through malls, scoping potential boyfriends-to-be. For years, the mall was simply a destination my mother efficiently and swiftly spirited me and my two sisters through at the beginning of each season. With pen and pad in hand, we'd have a pre-mall ritual. My mother would move from room to room in our house, taking notes on what each of our wardrobes lacked. My sisters and I were responsible for removing the contents of our drawers and uncovering whatever stained or outgrown T-shirts, shorts, pants, skirts, might need replacing. She'd discard the old clothes into waiting paper bags, which we dropped at the Salvation Army, and then she'd make notes on a piece of paper.

It was like assembly line shopping: regimented, economical. We'd each get a list: Something like: *Nina: shirts, long-sleeve (2); pants, lightweight (2); skirts, short/long (1); T-shirts (4)*. And then we'd head out, just the four of us, for a densely packed day of racing from store to store, scribbling the items off our list one by one. And just as our attentions, enthusiasms, or energy started to hit a treacherous low, we'd pause somewhere in the mix for a cookie or ice cream. Save for that momentary treat-induced sugar high, for the most part, those shopping adventures were a get-the-job-done kind of affair.

It took me years to reclaim the mall as a place for generating ideas, spending leisure time, *chilling*. In grade school, my friends and I started to shop socially. We would take the bus to San Francisco's Stonestown Galleria, or downtown's Union Square to meet up. Oftentimes, I might return with a headband or a cream I'd end up using once; I'd become a casualty of the enticing lure of chrome packaging or

who knew?

Looking for patterns to follow? Head over to www.voguepatterns.com, where you can order the classy magazine, filled with great, easy-to-follow instructions for a big discount.

cool overhead techno music. But I got in the habit of hiding my purchases so as not to have to own up to my impulsive decisions—my often ridiculous overpriced loot.

Soon enough, I got to think of the mall, or shopping district, like any other American teen. It became my meeting place, my hangout. I'd pick up free samples of new products, so many in fact, that I never needed to buy anything at all. Whenever the sample ran out, I'd just pop open a new one.

Years later, it remains a place I head to seek refuge, to do (*ahem*) research. I truly do think of it as that; stores comprise pages of a visual book to be read and from which to learn.

These days, I still have a soft spot in my heart for malls. A day at the mall makes me feel like I'm living in one big stack of catalogues; a huge house filled with someone else's clothes in which I can play dress-up; a fanciful playland. Oftentimes, I'll kill a few hours, think through some personal problems, and spend no more than a few dollars on an iced coffee.

With several hours free, I'll find myself heading out to one of my favorite malls. In Boston, that's usually the Chestnut Hill mall, which is filled with energetic aging lounge singers; registering brides-to-be; and nary a pants-sagger in sight. I'll park outside, turn off my brain and choose a route to wander: downstairs left, upstairs left, upstairs right, downstairs right.

Greeted by an inviting spread of *TRY ME!* tester tubes at a cosmetics store, I'll take the employees up on the offer, smoothing dabs of cream on the top of my hand, testing lipstick colors on the inside of my palm, spritzing perfume a few inches from my nose and quickly poking my head out to sniff. A bright cherry-red lipstick might remind me of a look I saw in a magazine, and I must know if, combined with my fine features and fair complexion, I am truly transformed into the coy sexpot the latest glossy has promised.

At a shoe store, I'll slide my small, narrow feet into the displays that are often exactly my size. Wildly provocative heels; a décolleté on the toe; strappy high sandals—I'll try it all, prancing around, lifting up my hemline to see what the shoes do to my ankles, my calves, my look.

I'll breeze through a clothing store and run my hands along various fabrics, lightly caressing a lace cuff, rubbing the sleeve of a velour track suit, delicately touching an exquisite brushed twill. Without meaning to, they get incorporated into my mental Rolodex of fabric feelings.

In college, I turned shopping into a reward. After finishing a chapter of *Ulysses*, or pounding out the rough draft of a paper on the significance of thrift store shopping for a cultural criticism class, I'd hop onto a train heading downtown to SoHo or NoLita, perhaps even farther south to Century 21. When I was first acclimating myself to the city, I'd get off at a new subway stop each time to teach myself new areas, discover new shops. Wandering the streets, popping in and out of boutiques, and taking time out on some random stoop to people-watch was one way that I would teach myself both about the city and about fashion. I'd look, incorporate, and head home to revise what I already had.

Shopping districts, streets dotted with character-filled boutiques— these are the places to which I'm drawn. And I'll drag whomever I'm with or simply head off on my own.

I'll occasionally buy something during these all-too-frequent afternoon shopping escapades. But more often than not, my mall adventure is simply just that. A time of gathering ideas, of fancying things, of touching, and of trying on. Even when I walk away empty-handed— which is most times—I return to my own closet bursting with creative new ideas, ways to refashion what I already have and revise my repertoire. I'll perhaps layer a shirt over a tank top in a new way; I'll pair a new belt with a skirt; I'll roll up the cuffs on a jacket to a sporty elbow length. I'll learn how to be more chic while still being cheap.

Some girls are better than I about shopping without spending, about getting ideas without losing too much cash. To be sure, I can certainly play the shopping sucker, falling hard for pearly-white peach-scented creams ($15.99), setting my heart on yet another pair of Mary Janes ($68, but the strap is so different on this pair!), or another black belt I don't really need ($20). I like to chalk it up as simply one of the perils I undertake all in the name of research, of assembling all the components of this pseudo-luxury lifestyle. Join me!

the books

Urban Girls would be nothing without the assistance of books—and lots of 'em. I looted these books for all sorts of useful nuggets. We must pay tribute. Thanks, guys!

Andrea Immer's Wine Buying Guide for Everyone, Andrea Immer. Broadway Books, 2002.

Best Dressed, Suzy Gershman. Three Rivers Press, 2000.

Bobbi Brown Beauty, Bobbi Brown and Anne Marie Iverson. Harper Perennial, 1998.

Chic Simple Clothes, Jeff Stone and Christa Worthington. Knopf, 1993.

The Complete Idiot's Guide to Successful Dressing, Karyn Repinski. MacMillan, 1998.

The Cook and the Gardener: A Year of Recipes and Writings from the French Countryside, Amanda Hesser. W.W. Norton & Co., 2000.

Don't Go to the Cosmetics Counter Without Me, Paula Begoun. Beginning Press, 2000.

Dress Like a Million, Leah Feldon. iUniverse.com, 2001 Distribution, 1998.

The Fashion Book. Phaidon Press Inc., 2001.

Fraud, David Rakoff. Broadway Books, 2002.

The Good Egg: More than 200 Fresh Approaches from Soup to Dessert, Marie Simmons. Houghton Mifflin, 2000.

Home Comforts: The Art & Science of Keeping House, Cheryl Mendelson. Scribner, 1999.

House & Garden's Decorating With Plants. Pantheon Books, 1978.

James Beard's Cookbook 3rd Edition, James A. Beard. Marlowe & Co, 2002.

The Joseph H. Pilates Method At Home, Eleanor McKenzie. Ulysses Press, 2000.

The Leopard Hat, Valerie Steiker. Pantheon Books, 2002.

Leslie Linsley's High-Style Low-Cost Decorating Ideas For Every Room In the House, Leslie Linsley. Griffin Trade Paperback, 1999.

My Misspent Youth, Megan Daum. Open City Books, 2001.

Never Pay Retail, Sid Kirchheimer. Rodale Press, 1996.

A New Way to Cook, Sally Schneider. Artisan, 2001.

Secrets From the Underground Shopper, Sue Goldstein. Taylor Pub, 1986.

Shopping for Furniture: A Consumer's Guide, Leonard Bruce Lewin. Linden, 1998.

The Tipping Point, Malcolm Gladwell. Little, Brown & Company, 2000.

Why We Buy: The Science of Shopping, Paco Underhill. Simon & Schuster, 1999.

the index

the author

Photo by Tess Steinkolk

Nina Willdorf has written for *Glamour*, the *New York Post*, *Entertainment Weekly*, *Teen Vogue*, and *Blender* on style, health, entertainment, and popular culture. Nina has previously held jobs at the *Boston Phoenix*, the *New York Observer*, *Worth* magazine, the *Chronicle of Higher Education*, and *Health* magazine, bouncing between San Francisco, Washington, D.C., Boston, and New York, where she currently works as a Senior Associate Editor at *Child* magazine and lives the luxe life on less. For more on Nina, visit www.ninawilldorf.com.